Crewel & Surface Embroidery
INSPIRATIONAL FLORAL DESIGNS

Trish Burr

SALLYMILNER
PUBLISHING

FOR MY DAUGHTERS, STACEY, TESSA AND KATIE, WITH ALL MY LOVE.

'He hath made everything beautiful in his time' (Eccl. 3:11).

First published in 2008 by
Sally Milner Publishing Pty Ltd
734 Woodville Road
Binda NSW 2583 AUSTRALIA

© Trish Burr 2008
Reprinted 2009

Design: Anna Warren, Warren Ventures
Editing: Anne Savage
Photography: Tim Connolly

Printed in China

National Library of Australia Cataloguing-in-Publication data:

Burr, Trish.
    Crewel & surface embroidery : inspirational floral designs.

    ISBN 9781863513777 (pbk.).

    1. Crewelwork. 2. Embroidery. 3. Flowers in art. I.
    Title. (Series : Milner craft series).

    746.44

Disclaimer
Information and instructions given in this book are presented in good faith, but no warranty is given nor results guaranteed, nor is freedom from any patent to be inferred. As we have no control over physical conditions surrounding application of information herein contained in this book, the author and publisher disclaim any liability for untoward results.

10 9 8 7 6 5 4 3 2

ACKNOWLEDGEMENTS

A grateful heart a garden is,
Where there is always room
For every lovely, Godlike grace
To come to perfect bloom.
ETHEL WASGATT DENNIS

There are numerous people who help behind the scenes in the compilation of a book and this one has been no exception—in fact, looking back at the number of people who have been involved makes me realise how much I have to be grateful for.

To Anne Frazier of Gloriana Threads and Julie of Gumnut Yarns for providing threads free of charge for this book, and to Robyn and Noel of Cascade House and Caron Collection for providing discounted threads. It is such a pleasure to work with such superb yarns. To Marian at the Crewel Gobelin for her assistance in purchasing the numerous other thread brands that she stocks. I have never before received parcels of thread so beautifully packed and laid out! To Judie at Thistle Needleworks and Joey at the Twining Thread for all your help in purchasing thread and fabric supplies.

To Gretchen Cagle, President of Gretchen Cagle Publications, Inc, in Claremore, Oklahoma, for granting permission to use extracts of her exquisite decorative paintings for interpretation into embroidery. Her remarkable use of colour and shading inspired many of the colour schemes used in my projects. Gretchen has received numerous awards for her work and her books, together with those of other master decorative painters, are available from her website: http://www.gretchencagle.com.

To Country Bumpkin Publications for the beautiful wool embroidery projects portrayed in *Inspirations* magazine and the book *The World's Most Beautiful Embroidered Blankets*. These projects, embroidered by the world's most talented needleworkers, inspired the use of small flower motifs in my bouquets. To Margie and Marian, my grateful thanks for granting permission to copy some of the superb illustrations and instructions from *The World's Most Beautiful Embroidered Blankets*: page 70, gypsophila;

page 104, large rosebud, flower blossom, wheat, and fly stitch leaf; page 113, blue daisy and lavender spray.

To all at Sally Milner—Ian Webster, Libby Renney, Penny Doust—and Anne Savage, the designers, photographer and all those behind the scenes, who make it possible to produce such first-rate publications.

To my daughters—Stacey, for the hours of work she put into the beautiful coloured stitch diagrams, and Tess, who coloured in the last few to help out when the pressure was on, thanks, my girls. To Glynn for the time and effort put into the computer illustrations, much appreciated.

To my regular Friday stitching group and my students for your encouragement and honest opinions—it was such a help, thank you. To Cory for the gift of the lovely antique linen which I so enjoyed using. To my dear friend Pat Raven who sent over essential items from the UK (and always in a hurry!)—you are such a great help Pat, thank you as always. Janey Cramp in New Zealand, your poppy is here—a reminder of our special time together. Lou Sheers, I could not leave you out—your encouragement was just what I needed to get to the finish line. To my family in Zimbabwe, New Zealand, Australia—all of you, for your support and encouragement at all times. To my husband Simon, and daughters Stacey, Tessa and Katie, for helping me to stay focused on what is important, reassuring me when I get frantic as deadlines loom, reminding me that I have threads attached to my trousers when leaving the house and supporting my creative endeavours—I love you all.

CONTENTS

INTRODUCTION

In the course of the embroidery classes I have given over the last year or so it became apparent there was a growing need for projects that were less time consuming and could be more easily fitted into today's busy lifestyles. Most of my students admitted to having started at least one project that had been shelved when they moved onto something else because the first was taking so long to complete that they had become bored. I resolved to design a series of projects that would cover the fabric more quickly than one strand of cotton, were challenging but not overwhelming, decorative but also practical, with pleasing colour schemes. This began the search for an original style of embroidery that expressed my love of soft shading with floral design.

After much trial and error, sleepless nights and driving my family mad with 'What do you think of this?', 'What do you think of that?', I finally produced a floral bouquet that incorporated all the elements I wanted to express. Unlike the solitary botanical subjects that graced the pages of my previous two books, *Redouté's Finest Flowers in Embroidery* and *Long and Short Stitch Embroidery: A Collection of Flowers*, these projects are more stylised, allowing for artistic licence and conferring a freedom of expression. My inspiration came from the art of master decorative painters in the United States and Australia, and from Russia's Zhostovo folk art style.

I was just itching to find an excuse to use the gorgeous ranges of silk, wool and cotton overdyed and space-dyed threads on the market, so I decided to try incorporating them into designs with smaller motifs and finer details. The results were exciting and gave me the confidence to blend space-dyed threads into shaded motifs and to combine silk, wool and cotton to produce interesting textural variations. I love this new form of embroidery and feel as though I have a warehouse of ideas at my disposal just waiting to be painted with thread on fabric.

I am often asked 'Where do you find the time?' The answer is that you don't *find* the time, you *make* it. If you try to find it you never will. Sometimes this means sitting up late at night or slotting in a few stitches while the dinner is cooking, or getting the chores done a bit earlier in the morning to free up time later.

The aim of this book is to provide achievable projects that are not too time consuming. I have tried to use the minimum of stitches with clear illustrations and good explanations so that you can easily follow the methods outlined.

I like to think that we never stop learning, that if we are open to new ideas and have the courage to break the boundaries of conventional methods we allow others to find the freedom to follow suit. As spiritual activist and founder of The Peace Alliance, Marianne Williamson, once said, 'Playing small does not serve the world. As we let our own Light shine, we unconsciously give other people permission to do the same.' It has given me so much pleasure to compile these projects and it is my hope that they will motivate you to create many beautiful embroideries and let your own Light shine!

MATERIALS AND EQUIPMENT

FABRIC

The traditional fabric used for crewel embroidery is linen twill, available in a natural honey colour or oyster white. For these projects you need a fabric that is suitable for both crewel and surface embroidery, and for this purpose linen remains the best choice as it gives way to the needle and closes up around the holes afterwards. My fabrics of choice are either linen union, with a backing of iron-on interfacing, or Belgian linen. If you are unable to obtain either of these you can substitute with a furnishing-weight fabric containing some degree of linen if possible (say, 50% cotton–50% linen) or any similar medium-weight fabric that has a close weave and little or no stretch in it. Fine surface-embroidery fabrics will not be suitable: the fabric needs to be of medium weight to support this type of embroidery.

The weave needs to be close so that you have a choice of stitch placement, and not stretchy, otherwise the fabric can become overstretched in the hoop or frame, resulting in distortion when removed. Silk fabric such as silk dupion or any slub silk is fine, it is best not to use synthetic fabrics.

Whatever fabric you choose to use, be sure to wash it in very hot water and iron it to pre-shrink it before use.

SUGGESTED FABRICS Pure linen twill, linen union, Belgian linen, Graziano 'Ricamo' linen, 32/40 count linen.

NOTE If you use DMC stranded cotton only, you can use a finer linen fabric.

THREADS

There is a plethora of thread brands on the market, and those I list here are just a few of the yarns that I was able to sample. (I was in my element!) I have had the most wonderful time trying out different combinations of thread and come to the conclusion that we are limited only by our imagination. Two combinations I found worked successfully were wool with cotton, and wool with silk; not only did the different textures contrast beautifully but the range of colours also enabled me to mix the exact shade I was looking for.

Thread equivalents

I should mention here that if you are unable to obtain any of the exotic threads I have used, the projects can all be easily worked using DMC stranded cotton or a mix of DMC cotton and Appleton wool.

It is important when you mix stranded cotton and wool to use the correct fabric. The fabric needs to be dense enough that the wool does not sit on top of it, and yet fine enough to allow the use of one strand of cotton when necessary. Belgian linen, linen twill and linen union are all suitable

The threads I have used in these projects include:

Wools

APPLETON CREWEL WOOL: A medium 2-ply yarn that comes in a wide variety of colours (about 420) and is particularly suitable for shading. The colour range includes the vintage shades that other ranges do not include and which are so necessary for this type of embroidery.

CASCADE HOUSE SHADED CREWEL WOOL: A 2-ply crewel wool that comes in a good range of approximately 200 shades. It is made from the finest merino wool, is smooth and even, and a pleasure to stitch with. The colours are slightly shaded, which can create an interesting effect.

GLORIANA LORIKEET SPACE-DYED CREWEL WOOL: This is superb. It is a 9-ply yarn so you can separate the plies and use as many as you want. It is made from the finest Australian wool and is lovely to stitch with. The vintage colour range is gorgeous (around 190 colours) and only slightly variegated, so it is possible to shade with them. I hope to see this range expanded in the near future!

GUMNUT CREWEL WOOL 'BLOSSOMS' AND 'DAISIES': A gently shaded crewel wool that comes in a good range of around 282 colours. The Blossoms range is slightly thicker than Appleton crewel wool, while Daisies is finer. Both are made from the finest Australian wool which is silky and lovely to stitch with, and include some unique colours, especially in the range of greens and golds. I would like to see the Daisies range expanded in the future.

PATERNA PERSIAN WOOL: A 100% virgin stranded wool that comes in a wonderful range of 418 colours. It is thicker than Appleton, but can be used successfully for heavier motifs.

Silks

CARON WATERLILIES: A lovely selection of space-dyed colours that can be used for background elements or in combination with wool.

GLORIANA 12-PLY SILK: Again a lovely array of space-dyed colours that are superb to stitch with as they do not slip or catch on your fingers. They are particularly effective when used on top of or in combination with wool.

GUMNUT STARS: A lovely range of stranded silk available in approximately 150 gently shaded colours.

NB When using silk ensure you check for colourfastness and follow the directions for washing.

Stranded cottons

DMC 6-STRANDED COTTON: Comes in a wonderful array of colours (about 450) and can be used alone or in combination with wool.

ANCHOR 6-STRANDED COTTON: Comes in a good array of colours (about 400) and can be used alone or in combination with wool.

CARON WATERCOLOURS: Comes in a wonderful array of variegated colours (approximately 215). It is a hand-dyed 3-strand pima cotton with a silky sheen which is equivalent in weight to one strand of Paterna Persian wool or 6 strands of stranded cotton. It is a bit on the thick side but can be used successfully alone for background elements.

Metallic thread

There are many brands available. I have used mainly DMC and Kreinik, in small amounts, but as long as the colour is the same you could use just about anything.

Other yarns

CHAMELEON PERLE THREAD: A perle cotton available in approximately 100 lovely colours which could be used as substitutes for any of the perle yarns used in this book.

GUMNUT YARNS 'BUDS': A perle silk available in 150 colours. It is lovely to work with, glides through the fabric and is particularly suitable for background elements, French knots and bullions.

HOUSE OF EMBROIDERY PERLE: A perle cotton available in about 210 lovely colours which could be used as substitutes for any of the perle yarns used in this book

Shade card

Get yourself a shade card for the brand of thread you are using; it will prove an invaluable tool when choosing colours. Try to use a brand that has a good colour selection as you can never have too many colours for this style of embroidery.

HOOPS AND FRAMES

An embroidery hoop or frame is essential for this type of embroidery, as it is imperative that the fabric be kept very taut as you work to prevent distortion.

Hoops

A wooden hoop, also known as a tambour or ring, is made up of two hoops, one inside the other, the outer hoop having a screw for tightening the fabric. It is best to use a deep-sided hoop, similar to the kind used for quilting. Hoops are available in different sizes; use the smallest hoop that you can without encroaching too much on the design. The border between the design and the hoop edge should be a minimum of 2 cm (^{3}⁄$_4$ in).

To avoid the risk of a dirty 'ring mark' being left on your work it is recommended that you bind all hoops before putting the embroidery fabric in place. To do this take bias binding (opened out flat) or a narrow strip of waste cotton fabric and bind it around the inner hoop, catching the end with a couple of stitches to prevent slipping. Alternatively, you can place a piece of white tissue paper over the area before replacing the outer ring, then tear away the tissue paper from the working area, leaving a ring around the edge.

Place the fabric (with iron-on interfacing pre-applied where required) over the inner hoop, place the outer hoop on top and push down. Tighten the fabric as much as possible and then adjust the screw until drum tight.

It is not advisable to use a hoop when stitching with silk thread unless the silk is washable, as it may be difficult to remove the ring marks. Use a frame instead. Remove the hoop at the end of each stitching session to prevent ring marks, which may be difficult to remove, developing on any fabric.

When you have tightened the fabric in the hoop as much as possible, hold it over the steam from a kettle until just damp. Allow to dry and the fabric will become drum tight.

Frames

My preference is for an artist's four-sided canvas stretcher frame. These can be bought unassembled in various sizes at any good art shop; this enables you to make up the specific size you need.

Centre the fabric over the front of the frame and secure with drawing pins, easing the fabric into place so that it is taut over the frame. There are various types of frames on the market and the choice is dependent upon trial and error and what suits you best. Frames have the added advantages over hoops of keeping your fabric taut without developing weakened areas caused by screw openings, and of not leaving ring marks. When you have completed the stitching you can leave the work on the frame, wash it in mild soapy water and leave till dry—your work will lie beautifully flat without any distortion or puckering.

Scissors

You will need a small, sharp pair of embroidery scissors for cutting threads. It is worth spending a little extra and getting the best pair that you can afford. Be brutal in your resolution to keep your embroidery scissors for cutting threads only— not fabric, not paper, not anything else. This is a constant

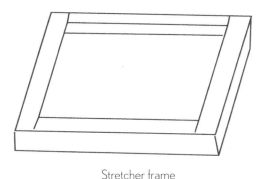

Stretcher frame

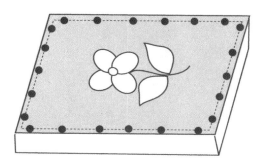

Fabric stretched and tacked onto frame

bone of contention in my house—even now, after years of threatening dire retribution, I far too often find my precious scissors blunt and covered with glue, having been misappropriated for use on thick cardboard homework projects!

NEEDLES

Chenille or crewel needles should be used for this style of embroidery. The larger the number the smaller the needle. While you need to work with the one that suits you best, here is a guideline:

* Crewel/embroidery needle size 4 for crewel wool and other yarns of similar weight
* Crewel/embroidery needle size 8 or 9 for fine wool or two strands of cotton
* Crewel/embroidery needle size 10 for one strand of cotton or fine silk
* Chenille needle size 26 for crewel wool

I find embroidery needles sizes 4 and 9 suitable for most of my work. Always buy a good-quality recognised brand of needle and change it as soon as it becomes tarnished or difficult to pull through the fabric. You may wish to use a milliner's needle for bullion stitch but I find my crewel size 9 is fine.

PENS AND PENCILS

Water-soluble pens are not suitable for fine work as the lines they make are too thick, but they could be used for crewel work. Be very careful when using them, for although the colour may appear to have washed out, the lines can reappear when dry.

When using a pencil to draw on to your fabric it is advisable to use a fairly hard lead pencil. A Berol Verifine lead pencil in white can be used for dark fabrics. If the fabric you are using is textured it may be difficult to obtain a smooth line with a hard pencil, in which case you can use a softer one such as an HB. These pencils are available at any good art shop.

I also use a very fine black permanent marker such as a Pigma Micron 01 for clear lines. Be careful that you stitch slightly to the outside of these lines to cover them adequately.

TECHNIQUES

PREPARING THE FABRIC

It is best to wash your fabric first in hot water to pre-shrink it and remove any dirty marks, then iron with a steam iron. Always choose the best quality fabric you can afford and cut a generous size to allow for mounting or making up, leave an allowance of at least 10 cm (4 in) around the design.

Grain of the fabric

Find the grain of the fabric by pulling out a thread on two sides at right angles to each other, so that the grain is lined up before mounting and stitching. This will prevent distortion of work when completed.

TRANSFERRING A DESIGN

Outlines for transferring the designs are supplied for each project; they can be used actual size, or reduced or enlarged according to your personal preference. The easiest way to do this is by photocopying. Do remember that if you reduce a design in size, the number of embroidery stitches will also be reduced, and could limit the shading that can be applied, just as enlarging a design will increase the number of stitches

needed to fill the outlines. You cannot reduce or enlarge the actual stitch size, as this will give a very uneven finish. Remember to increase the size of the background fabric if you choose to enlarge a design.

There are a number of ways to transfer a design onto fabric, but by far the easiest is to place the fabric on top of the design, with a light source behind the design, and trace over the design with an HB pencil.

Tracing methods

* Use a light box.
* Place a light under a glass table.
* Hold fabric and design up against a glass window (you will need to attach both with masking tape to prevent movement).

Another method uses fabric carbon paper; in this case you place the carbon between the design and the fabric (design on top, fabric underneath) and draw over the design with a sharp pencil. Graphite carbon paper is the best type to use, but check at intervals to see that the lines are being transferred.

Directional lines

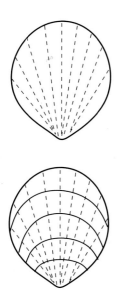

It is helpful to draw directional lines (guidelines) onto the fabric after transferring the design. These will help guide your stitches towards the base of the shape. Place the first guideline down the centre and work others on either side of this. You can put in as many guidelines as you like. The lines should radiate from the centre point of the shape outwards. You may wish to draw in horizontal guidelines as well, following the contours of the shape, to guide your rows of shading, but be careful that your rows do not become too regimented, causing hard lines of colour. You will have to encroach on some of the lines to give a staggered effect. Decide on the number of shades you are going to use on the motif and divide the motif equally to accommodate them.

Starting and ending off

There are many ways to secure your thread at the start of your work. After much trial and error I have found the method outlined here to be the most suitable, as it does not leave any lumps and bumps.

Starting off

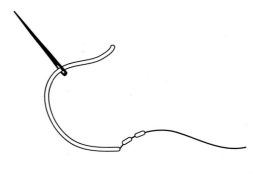

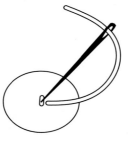

Make a few small running stitches in an area to be covered by embroidery or directly on the design line. Start about 10 mm (⅓ in) away from the point you wish to start and work the running stitches back towards this point. Leave a short tail of about 12 mm (½ in). Start stitching and these running stitches will be covered as you work.

Ending off

When ending off, work a few running stitches in a place to be covered as before, and cut off close to the fabric.

If you have run out of working space (in other words, the motif is completed) you can work your thread into the back of the work with a few small stitches. Try to catch some of the fabric while doing this to make sure it is very secure.

NB It is best not to carry your thread across long stretches at the back of the work. Rather, end off and start again.

COMPLETION OF WORK

Washing and pressing

If the work is clean, place it face down on a fluffy towel and press it on the back with a steam iron (this will not flatten the design). Do not slide the iron across the back of the work. If it is necessary to wash your work, double-check that you have used washable and colourfast threads and that your fabric is pre-shrunk. Work that does not meet these conditions cannot be washed as the fabric will shrink, causing massive puckering of the stitching and the thread colours to run—throw it in the dustbin and start again! Wash in tepid (lukewarm) water with a mild soap, rinse, and roll up in a fluffy towel. While still damp, place the work face down on the towel and press until dry.

If a design has been worked in crewel wool, it should be blocked rather than pressed (see below).

Blocking

If the work has become distorted or the fabric puckered, it may be necessary to block it, to stretch it back into shape. There are two ways of doing this.

Wash the work first (if necessary) and dry it. Take a square frame (or an upholstered frame) of suitable size and place the work on top of it, using small tacks or pins to fix two opposite sides to the frame. (A square frame is an artist's stretcher frame similar to the type used to frame a picture; an upholstered frame is covered in foam, then fabric. The fabric is stretched over a square frame and stapled directly into the wood, but on an upholstered frame the fabric is stretched across and pinned into the foam cover.) Stretch the fabric across until it is squarely on the frame and tack or pin the other two sides. Alternatively, you can use a piece of hardboard covered with dressmaker's graph paper. Line the fabric up squarely using the graph paper as a guide, and tack your work to the hardboard.

When the work is squarely and securely tacked in place, dampen the fabric with water in a mist sprayer, or hold the back of the fabric over a steaming kettle until damp. Leave it until it is completely dry (a couple of hours, or as long as necessary) and remove the tacks. The fabric will spring back into shape and the stitching will be smooth and even.

Mounting

If you would like to frame your work you can either take it to a professional framer who will stretch and mount it for you, or mount it and frame it yourself. This can be done using one of the self-adhesive mounting boards that are available especially for the purpose, or you can tape the work onto a piece of board with masking tape.

I asked my local framer how he mounted needlework and this is what he said: The fabric is dampened and then stretched onto a piece of mount board. It is then stapled around the edges with a staple gun or taped down with masking tape (depending on the weight of the fabric) and left to dry. This is the only method that ensures that there are no creases or puckers in the fabric.

1   Position the mount board centrally on the back of your design. Fold one edge of the fabric over and push pins through the fabric and board along one edge.

2   Stretching the fabric gently, pull it across to the opposite side, fold edge over and pin.

3   Starting from one end, lace the fabric from one side to the other, crossing the threads.

4   Now pin and lace the other two sides in the same manner. Fold in and slipstitch the corners. Once all four sides are laced, remove the pins. Your work should be taut and even.

Using the finished embroidery

There are some wonderful ideas online for making up your completed stitching or you can get ideas from stitching magazines (Inspirations magazine has some stunning ideas with clear instructions for making up) or purchase ready-made items. Here are some ideas for making up your completed stitching.

Small designs

Potpourri lavender sachet, pincushion, needle-case holder, cosmetic bag, notebook cover, spectacle case, scissor keeper, guest hand towel, centre pieces for quilt, small framed or mounted pictures, greeting cards.

Medium sized designs

Small cushions in various shapes and sizes, bolster cushion, linen bag, evening bag, hot water bottle cover, hand towel, embroidery accessory holder, armchair caddy, framed picture, centre piece border for quilt or blanket.

Large designs

Cushions in various shapes and sizes, tote/carry bag, framed picture, centre piece border for fire screen, blanket, quilt, wall hanging or bedcover.

Tips for working the designs

❁ Ensure that your fabric (and backing if applicable) are stretched tight in a frame. If your work loosens as you are stitching, re-position it to make it tighter.

❁ It is worth spending the extra time on preparing your embroidery—you don't want to put all that effort in and find it puckers in the end.

❁ Ensure that you work under a good light, preferably daylight. Consider purchasing a magnifier light to work under as it is much easier on the eyes—I could not do without mine! I have an ultra slim fluorescent magnifier light with a 17.5X magnification which enables me to stitch at any time of the day or night.

❁ Transfer the basic outlines only—you can add the details later. I like to use a very fine black Pigma Micron permanent pen for the main outlines but an HB pencil is fine.

❁ Before working a motif in long and short stitch, add in guidelines in pencil to help direct your stitching. You may also want to sketch in the darker shadows with your pencil to help you decide where they will lie. (This is where I cheat a lot!)

❁ When working rows of long and short stitch remember to go about three-quarters of the way back into the previous stitches so that the shade in the first row is peeping out from behind the second row, and so on, with each succeeding row. This allows you to fit in more shades.

❁ Most of the projects use more than one shade of colour in each row of long and short stitch. The shades may be stitched alternately, one colour next to each other, or sometimes worked in blocks of colour, changing to the next shade in the same row.

❁ If you find it difficult to include highlighted areas with your long and short stitch, go back and add them in afterwards by blending in a few straight stitches in the lightest shade. The same applies to the shadowed areas.

❁ To emphasise shadowed areas along the edge of a leaf or petal you can work a fine line in split or stem stitch close to the edge in a very dark shade, or you can make very small straight stitches towards the base of the line.

❁ Remember that the colours from the flower are reflected in the leaves, so add in a few straight stitches of a similar flower shade afterward as a highlight.

* Remember that the light falls from the top left on each project, so everything on the top left should be lighter and everything underneath a bit darker.

* Remember that flowers, leaves, stems, etc. are never one flat colour. If you look at them in the garden or a painting you will see that they reflect other shades from nearby elements. Shadows and highlights will also reflect different shades. For instance, red may look almost black or dark brown in shadow but quite pinkish in light.

* Start with the larger motifs in the centre. Work the motifs that are furthest back and then work forward. The small motifs can be stitched afterwards.

* Some of the larger motifs are worked using a combination of wool and cotton, or wool and silk; in these cases use one strand of each together in the needle. I have done this to mix the shade that I need if I can't find the exact shade in a range—for example, grey wool mixed with teal green cotton equals grey slate green.

* Some of the motifs are worked using wool first with silk or cotton worked on top. Make sure you always stitch the wool first, never the reverse.

* If the motif is quite small fill it with the base shade and work the other shade in straight stitches on top of this, leaving the first colour to peep out from behind.

* When using space-dyed thread try to choose a piece that has the shades you want in it. This may mean cutting a piece out of the middle but you can use the rest in other projects so it will never be wasted.

* Put your work aside and view it from afar at regular intervals. If there are any areas that do not seem to blend correctly, or somehow look wrong, you can go back and correct them. Remember that this type of embroidery looks more like an oil painting than a fine watercolour, so don't beat yourself up over the smoothness of your stitching or the correctness of your technique. The important thing is that you provide enough contrast in your shades to give dimension and that the overall effect is pleasing to the eye.

* Be prepared to spend time on each motif and don't rush your work. Tell yourself that you are going to make one beautiful project this month (or even this year!) and it will be worth a hundred mediocre projects.

* If you want to make something in a hurry, say as a gift for a friend's birthday, choose one of the smaller designs and be realistic about the time frame—or give your friend an IOU!

* Wherever possible use the best quality fabrics and threads that you can afford, for there is nothing more pleasurable than stitching with the best. Try not to skimp by using inferior brands. If you can't afford the real thing ask for birthday or Christmas gifts or do without a haircut!

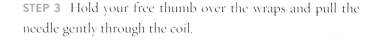

BULLION STITCH

STEP 1 Using 2 strands of thread and needle size 9 bring the needle up at A and down at B, then up again at A leaving a long loop.

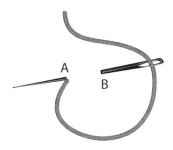

STEP 2 Wrap the thread gently around the needle in an anticlockwise direction the required number of times to create a coil. As a guide, 8 wraps for a short bullion, 18 wraps for a long bullion.

STEP 3 Hold your free thumb over the wraps and pull the needle gently through the coil.

STEP 4 Whilst pulling the thread, gently push down the top of the coil. Adjust coil as necessary until the bullion lies flat on the fabric.

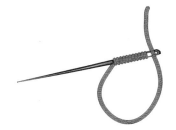

STEP 5 Insert the needle at B and pull through to complete the stitch.

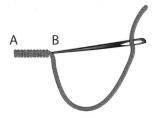

DETACHED CHAIN STITCH (LAZY DAISY STITCH)

This is a looped stitch which can be worked alone or in groups.

STEP 1 Bring the needle up through the fabric at A, back down very close to A and up again at B a short distance away (about 5 mm), looping the thread in an anti-clockwise direction under the tip of the needle.

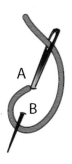

STEP 2 Pull the thread through at B over the loop.

STEP 3 Anchor down the stitch by taking it through to the back of the fabric. This completes the detached chain stitch.

STEP 4 Completed detached chain stitches around a circle.

FLY STITCH

This is an open detached chain stitch which when worked closed together can be used as a filling stitch for small leaves.

STEP 1 Bring the needle and thread up at A, back down at B and remerge at C, looping the thread under the tip of the needle as shown.

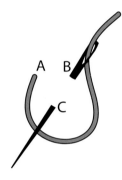

STEP 2 Pull the thread over the loop at C.

STEP 3 Anchor the stitch by taking it down to the back.

STEP 4 Working a leaf in fly stitch. Work the first fly stitch at the tip of the leaf, anchoring the stitch on the leaf stem. Work the second and subsequent fly stitches just below the first until the leaf shape is filled.

FRENCH KNOT

STEP 1 Using 2 strands of thread, bring the needle up at A. Wrap the thread around the needle once.

STEP 3 Pull the thread gently but quite firmly to form the knot against the fabric, then pull the needle through to the back of the fabric to complete the stitch.

STEP 2 Insert the needle tip into the fabric very close to A, but not into the same hole.

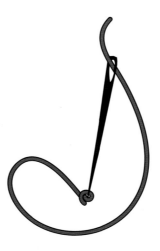

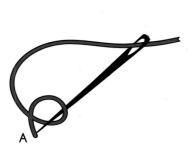

GRANITOS

These small stitches form a raised bunch which can be used as petals for small flowers.

STEP 1 Bring needle up at A and down at B.

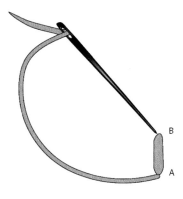

STEP 2 Completed first stitch.

STEP 3 Bring needle up at A in the same hole and down at B in the same hole. Pull the thread through, ensuring the stitch is positioned to the left of the first stitch.

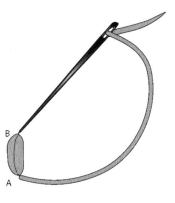

STEP 4 Completed second stitch.

STEP 5 Repeat as for the second stitch but position stitch to the right of the first stitch. Completed third stitch. Continue working in this way (about 4 or 5 stitches in total) until the granitos is complete.

LONG AND SHORT STITCH

Long and short stitch is also referred to as silk shading, soft shading, long and short shading or needlepainting, as the varying stitch lengths which encroach on each other lend this technique wonderfully to shading and give a realistic 'painted' finish. Long and short stitch is used as a filling stitch for all types of larger shapes. It is the most widely used stitch in this book and therefore worth spending time practising. There are a few ground rules for long and short stitch that we will explore in the techniques which follow; once you have mastered these we can look at ideas for enhancing the stitch by various means.

BASIC LONG AND SHORT STITCH

This is the basis of long and short stitch, worked in one direction only. It is quite often referred to as tapestry shading and can be used to fill in areas such as backgrounds. It is a good way to learn the stitch before embarking on the directional method.

STEP 1 Outline the edges of the shape with split stitch. (You can use stem stitch for a more raised outline.) Use 1 strand of the lightest shade of thread required for that element of the design to work the outline. (I have used a darker thread in the photograph for the purpose of demonstration.) The split stitch forms the foundation for the long and short stitch infill.

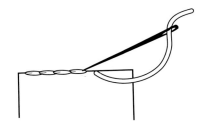

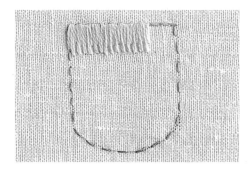

STEP 2 Work the first row in long and short stitch, using the lightest shade of thread. Bring the needle up at the outside edge and down into the fabric inside the shape, as this will ensure a neat even edge. Do not make your stitches too small, as this will give an uneven finish. The long stitches should be approximately 12 mm (½ in) in length and the short stitches about three-quarters of that length, 9 mm (³⁄₈ in).

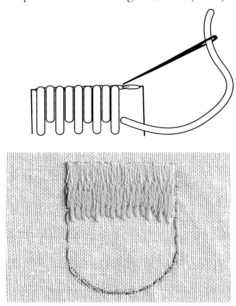

Work the second row in long stitch only, using the next darkest shade of thread. In this row bring the needle up through the fabric to split the ends of the previous stitches, and down into the fabric. Although these stitches are worked in long stitch only, vary their lengths slightly to give a soft uneven line, not a straight one. Long and short stitch is intended to produce a soft, blended effect, so avoid abrupt changes of tone.

STEP 3 Work the third and subsequent rows as for the second row. Continue to change the shades of thread to create a shaded look.

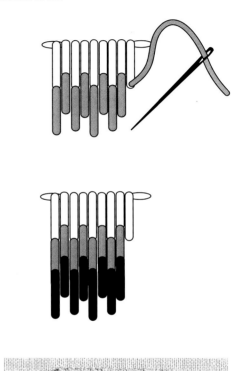

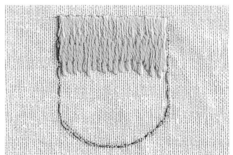

Directional long and short stitch

Filling a shape such as a petal

Shading does not always follow a straight course but can take different directions. If you study the structure of a petal, for example, you will see that it most often tapers towards the centre. The direction of stitches is most important and we need to know how to direct our stitches to follow the shape of a motif.

Long and short stitch is worked in five basic steps outlined below:

- ✿ Outline the motif to be stitched
- ✿ Draw directional guidelines into the shape.
- ✿ Work the foundation (first) row of long and short stitches
- ✿ Work the second row in staggered long stitches
- ✿ Complete the motif.

STEP 1 Select about 4 shades of yarn, from light to dark. Outline the shape with split or stem stitch with the lightest shade of yarn. Stem stitch will give a more padded raised edge. This edge will form the foundation for the shape to be worked.

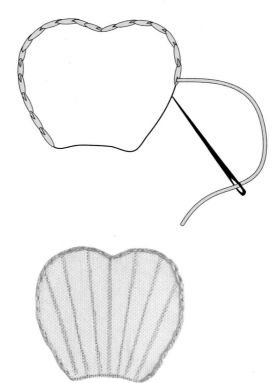

STEP 2   Pencil in the guidelines, drawing in the guideline down the centre of the motif, then splitting the halves in half again as shown. You can draw in as many lines as you need.

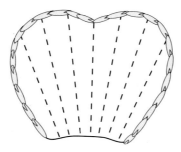

STEP 3   Work the first row in long and short stitch, using the lightest shade of thread. Start from the centre tip of the petal and work towards one side as shown. Come up in the shape and down over the split stitch edge—this allows you to control the stitches, resulting in a precise, neat border.

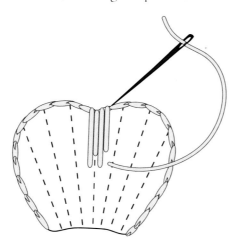

Shorten the stitch lengths when you reach the side to fit the curve. The stitches should be closely packed together with only a fibre between them so that the fabric is well covered, but not on top of each other so that they are overcrowded. This row forms the foundation for the successive rows, and needs to provide sufficient cover to work these rows into.

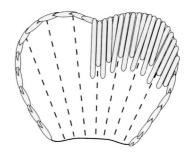

Add an extra small wedge stitch occasionally to adjust for the tapering shape. This stitch will subtly alter the direction of subsequent stitches.

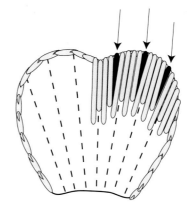

Remember to keep your stitches a good length, approximately 12 mm (½ in) for long stitches and 9 mm (⅜ in) for short stitches (when working in wool, lengthen these measurements slightly). If the stitches become too short the work will not look smooth.

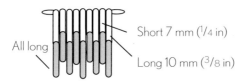

All long

Short 7 mm (¼ in)

Long 10 mm (³/8 in)

Complete the row by working from the centre tip towards the other side.

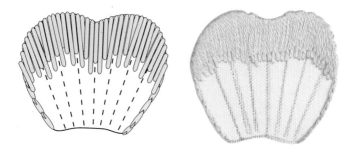

Tip

Think straight satin stitch when working the first row of long and short stitch. The only difference is that the stitches are staggered not even.

STEP 4 Work the second row in long stitch only, using the next darkest shade of thread. Again work from the centre out towards one side and then the other. (You may find it easier to turn your work around so that you are working into the shape.) Work every third or fourth stitch and then go back and fill in the gaps, keeping in line with the direction lines and reducing the amount of stitches if the shape narrows.

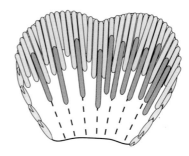

Follow the guidelines as closely as possible and work long stitches only, staggering each stitch and varying their lengths so that the row of stitching does not form a straight line.

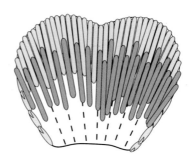

Split up through the ends of the stitches of the previous row (about one-third of the way back) and down into the motif. If necessary, split further back into some stitches to stagger them. Angle your needle close to the fabric when splitting up through the stitches to prevent holes forming.

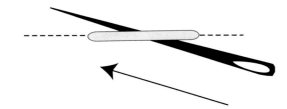

Complete the row as shown here.

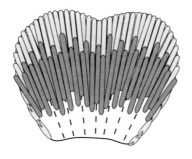

STEP 5 Subsequent rows—after the first row of long and short stitches is established, each succeeding row should be worked as for row two, and the stitches should be a similar length, but not regimented. No two stitches of the same length should lie next to each other—they should be staggered, creating an irregular line, so that the rows merge and encroach into each other.

Continue working each row, changing to the next shade of colour each time and reducing the number of stitches to fit the shape where necessary, until you reach the base of the motif. When you get to the last row the stitches will revert back to long and short.

Hold your work away from you and check there are no definite lines between shades. If there are, go back and add in a few long stitches here and there, tucking them in between existing stitches, to break up the line.

NOTE If you would like more in-depth information on this technique you may wish to refer to my previous book from Sally Milner Publishing, *Long and Short Stitch Embroidery: A Collection of Flowers.*

SATIN STITCH

This is a filling stitch used to fill small shapes.

STEP 1 Outline the shape with split stitch. This gives a nice neat, raised edge to your shape.

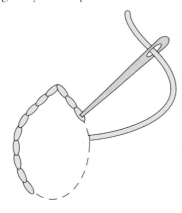

STEP 2 Start in the centre of the shape and work out on either side, angling the stitches across the shape as shown. Work stitches close together across the shape and over the split stitch edge, until it is filled.

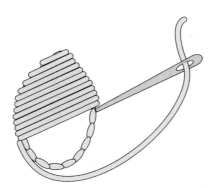

PADDED SATIN STITCH

STEP 1 Outline the shape with split stitch, then work a base of straight stitches across the shape in the opposite direction to the final covering satin stitches.

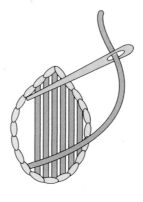

STEP 2 Work the satin stitch as before on top of the base of straight stitches.

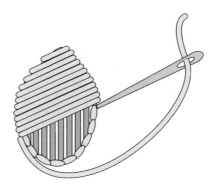

SPLIT STITCH

Split stitch is a variation of a simple backstitch, used to outline shapes and sometimes worked adjacently as a filling stitch for details such as stems. When used as a filling stitch it enables you to shade and change colour within very small spaces, and the results are amazing. This method has become my new preference for filling in smaller details such as stems as it gives more scope for shading in a restricted area.

Commencing with a backstitch, split each preceding stitch with the needle to form the next backstitch.

STEM STITCH

The stitches are worked from left to right and overlap each other, without splitting, to form a fine line. When worked adjacently they can be used to fill spaces such as stems and give a fine cord-like effect.

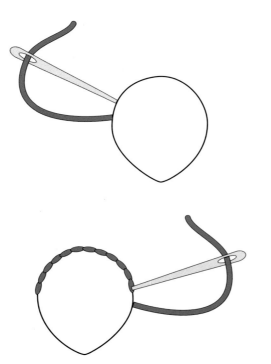

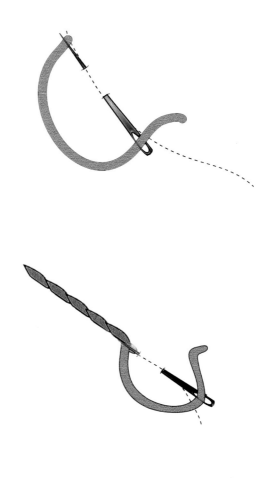

STRAIGHT STITCH

This stitch can be used to create either highlights or shadows when blended in on top of long and short stitch, or anywhere that straight stitches are required.

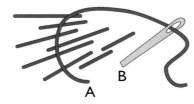

Bring the needle up at A and down at B. Make irregular straight stitches at intervals as shown.

INDIVIDUAL MOTIFS USED
IN BACKGROUNDS

BLOSSOM

This little blossom is used in the background of some of the projects. The method described here is the basic method of working it. It can be adapted for any other blossoms that are similar.

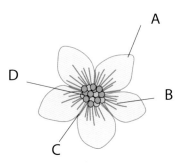

A   Fill petals using either a granitos for each or straight stitches from centre to tip. (When using straight stitches work from the same hole at base and fan out over tip.)

B   Work highlights in straight stitches from centre of flower into petals in a deeper shade using one strand of silk or cotton.

C   Work straight stitches in green between petals.

D   Work French knots using 2 strands of thread in centre.

DAISY

This little daisy is used in the background of some of the projects—this is the basic method of stitching it and can be adapted for any other daisies or similar flowers.

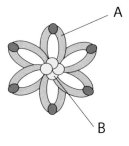

A   Stitch detached chain stitch petals around the centre of the flower.

B   Fill the centre with French knots using 2 strands of thread.

FLY STITCH LEAF

This little fly stitch leaf is used in the background of most of the projects. It can be adapted to fit leaves of any size or shape.

Starting at the tip of the leaf, work fly stitches close together one under the other until the leaf shape is filled.

GRASSES AND GYPSOPHILA

This is the method for stitching any of the grasses, gypsophila or similar that are used in the background of some of the projects. It can be adapted as necessary to fit the shape.

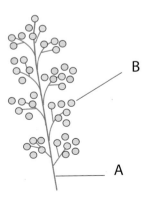

A Work the stems and little branches in split stitch.

B Scatter clusters of French knots around the branches using 2 strands of thread. (You can mix two different colours in the needle, or use wool and cotton, or wool and silk together for a different effect.)

LAVENDER

This little lavender stalk is used as a background element in many of the projects. This is the basic method for stitching any of the lavenders and can also be worked using one bullion instead of two.

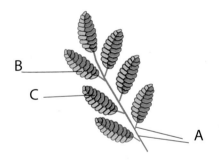

A Work the stems and little branches in split stitch.

B Work a bullion knot using about 7 wraps.

C Work a second bullion close to this using about 8 wraps so that it fits snugly next to the first bullion. (You can also make a little straight stitch between the bullions for a different effect.)

ROSEBUD

This little rosebud is used in many of the backgrounds of the projects. The method can be adapted to fit a rosebud of any size or shape. (If the rosebud is very small you can leave out the outer petals.)

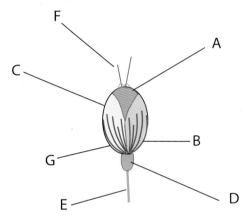

A Begin with a granitos of 7 stitches or fill with straight stitches. (If the rosebud is very large you can fill it with padded satin stitch from base to tip.)

B Embroider the second petal with three stitches across the lower section of the bud, using the same two holes and keeping the stitches to the right.

C Embroider the third petal in the same manner, working to the left.

D Work the calyx in straight or satin stitch.

E Work the stem in split stitch.

F At the tip of the bud embroider two tiny fly stitches with long anchoring stitches.

G Work a few straight stitches from base into bud.

WHEAT

This little head of wheat is used in the background of some of the projects.

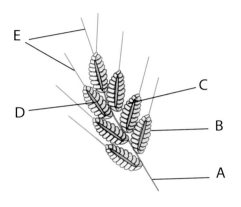

A Work the stem in split stitch.

B For each 'grain', work a bullion knot using about 7 wraps.

C Work a second bullion close to this using about 8 wraps so that it fits snugly next to the first bullion. (The second bullion should be a lighter shade than the first.)

D Work a straight stitch between the bullions in a darker shade.

E Work straight stitches from the end of the bullion out for the whiskers.

PRACTICE MOTIFS
STEP·BY·STEP

These four motifs are for practising before embarking on the projects.

SIMPLE PETAL

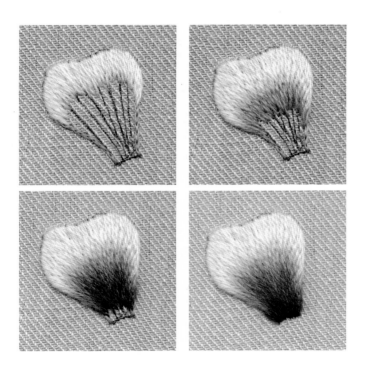

THREADS

Appleton crewel wool

white	991
pastel cream	871
pastel lilac	884
med mauve	603
med mauve	604
dark mauve	606

DMC stranded cotton

very dark bright plum	154

METHOD

Draw in guidelines. Outline petal with split stitch in one strand of 884. Fill with long and short stitch from the outside edge in towards the centre, in one strand of yarn, as follows: row 1 = 991; row 2 = 871; row 3 = 884; row 4 = 603; row 5 = 604; row 6 = 606. Finish with row 7 = DMC 154.

PETAL WITH TURNOVER

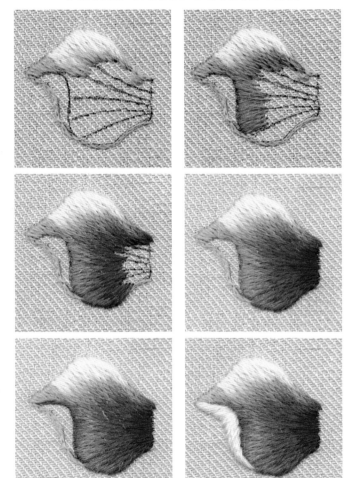

THREADS

Appleton crewel wool

pastel cream	871
pastel lilac	884
light mauve	602
med dull rose pink	144
med dark dull rose pink	145
dark rose pink	757

DMC stranded cotton

dark rose red	814
dark coffee brown	3860
very dark coffee brown	779

METHOD

Draw in guidelines. Outline petal with split stitch in one strand of 884. Fill with long and short stitch from the outside edge in towards the centre, using one strand of yarn at a time, as follows: row 1 = 871 alternating with 884; row 2 = 602, 144; row 3 = 145; row 4 = 757; row 5 = DMC 814.

Underline the turnover with split stitch using one strand of DMC 779. Work straight stitches towards and over the split stitch line in DMC 3860 to create a shadow. Outline the turnover with one strand of cream wool and fill with satin stitch over the split stitch edge.

Simple leaf

THREADS

Appleton crewel wool

pastel green	871
pale grey green	351
light mid olive green	342
med mid olive green	344
dark mid olive green	346

DMC stranded cotton

very dark brown	3371

METHOD

Draw in guidelines. Outline leaf with split stitch in one strand of 342, leaving the centre vein unworked. Always work from the outside edge in towards the centre vein.

Fill the leaf as follows using one strand of wool:

Left side: row 1 = 871 alternating with 351; row 2 = 351; row 3 = 342; row 4 = 344; row 5 = 346.

Right side: row 1 = 346 alternating with 344, 342, 351; row 2 = 344; row 3 = 342; row 4 = 351.

Work the centre vein in split stitch using one strand of DMC 3371.

LEAF IN WOOL WITH SILK OR COTTON HIGHLIGHTS

THREADS

Appleton crewel wool

pale grey green	351
pale peacock blue	641
light peacock blue	642
med mid blue	155
dark mid blue	157

DMC stranded cotton

med plum	3041
dark plum	3740
ecru	
light golden brown	613
dark coffee brown	779

METHOD

Draw in guidelines. Outline leaf with split stitch in one strand of 642, leaving the centre vein unworked. Always work from the outside edge in towards the centre vein.

Fill the leaf as follows using one strand of wool:

Top side: row 1 = 351 alternating with 641, 642; row 2 = 641 alternating with 642; row 3 = 155; row 4 = 157.

Bottom side: row 1 = 157 alternating with 155; row 2 = 155, 642; row 3 = 641; row 4 = 351.

Highlights: blend in straight stitches at the top of the leaf and in the centre as shown using DMC ecru and 613 alternately.

Shadows: blend in straight stitches at the base of the leaf as shown using DMC 3041 and 3740 alternately.

THE PROJECTS

Note Any of these projects can be stitched using DMC stranded cotton or Appleton crewel wool as alternatives for the exotic wool, cotton and silk threads.

THREAD EQUIVALENTS

If you want to substitute the threads used for each project please refer to the manufacturer's shade chart for similar colours. The charts are downloadable or viewable on the Internet, or available from the supplier or from your local needlework shop. If you are unable to obtain any of the space-dyed silks, wools or cottons they can be substituted with the nearest solid colours in Appleton crewel wool or DMC cotton. I have given alternatives in the first five projects.

PROJECT INSTRUCTIONS

A numbered stitch diagram is provided with a corresponding abbreviation key which should enable you to see at a glance what needs to be done without having to flip through pages. Detailed instructions follow.

GUIDE TO PREPARATION AND TRANSFER OF DESIGNS

❋ Cut a piece of fabric the size of the outline plus an extra 12 cm (4¹⁄₂ in) minimum all round.

❋ Pull a thread at right angles to find the straight grain of the fabric.

❋ Wash and iron the fabric.

❋ Bind the edges of the fabric either on a sewing machine or with masking tape.

❋ Copy the design by your preferred method from the tracing outline.

❋ Trace the outline onto the fabric using either a light source or carbon paper.

❋ Draw in guidelines with a pencil, for each motif before you stitch it. Note that the tracing lines for the smaller motifs are placement marks only as a guide to where the motif should be stitched.

❋ Mount your fabric into a hoop or frame, aligning the straight edges to the frame.

PROJECT 1: STEP-BY-STEP POPPY, BLOSSOMS AND BUDS

This project is stitched on natural Belgian linen with a medium iron-on interfacing to stabilise the fabric.

Permission granted by Gretchen Cagle Publications, Inc. for adaptation of Gretchen Cagle's design, 'A painter's legacy', previously published in *Heart to Heart: Forever Always* (copyright 1999).

THREAD KEY

DMC stranded cotton

pale gold	3047	ecru	ecru	med plum	3041	
light green gold	3013	light grey green	524	dark bright plum	3834	
med green gold	3012	med grey green	522	very dark bright plum	154	
dark green gold	3011	dark grey green	3363	dark brown	838	
aubergine	3860	blanc	blanc	very dark brown	3371	
dark aubergine	779	pale plum	3743	cream	3823	
		pale lavender	3747	pale gold	677	
		light plum	3042	light gold	676	
				med gold	729	
				dark gold	782	
				very dark gold	780	
				coffee brown	3790	

Caron Watercolours cotton

moonglow   146 (or DMC blanc)

Gloriana silk

ollalieberry   153
    (or DMC shades of plum; 3740 3041 3835)

Tracing outline

METHOD

Copy the design onto the fabric by your preferred method from the tracing outline.

1 Back gold-green leaf

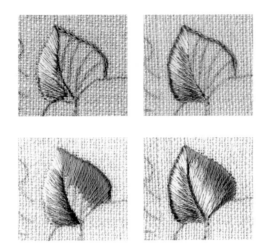

Outline the leaf in split stitch using 2 strands of med green gold 3012.

Fill the left side with long and short stitch, shading from light to dark, from the outside in towards the centre vein as follows:

One strand each of 3047 + 3013 and 3013 + 3012 (2 strands together in the needle) in the first row.

Change to one strand only in the next rows. Blend 3012 and 3860 into the next row.

Fill the right side from dark to light as follows:

One strand each of 3860 + 3011 and 2 strands of 3012 (2 strands together) in the first row.

Change to one strand only in the next rows. Blend 3012 and 3013 into the next row.

Blend 3047 into the next row.

Stitch the centre vein in split stitch using one strand of 779.

Stitch direction diagram

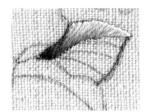 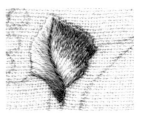

Outline the leaf in split stitch using 2 strands of med grey green 522.

Fill the left side with long and short stitch shading from light to dark, from the outside in towards the centre vein as follows:

One strand each ecru — 524 (2 strands together) in the first row.

Change to one strand for the next rows. Blend in 522 and 860 into the next row.

Blend in 3860 and 779 for the shadows towards the base.

Fill the right side from dark to light as follows:

One strand each 3860 — 779 and 3363 — 3860 and 3363 (2 strands together) in the first row.

Change to one strand for the next rows. Blend in 522 and 524 into the next row.

Blend in ecru into the next row.

Stitch the centre vein in split stitch using one strand of 779.

3 Bottom left grey-green leaf

Outline the leaf in split stitch using 2 strands of med grey green 522.

Fill the left side with long and short stitch shading from light to dark, from the outside in towards the centre vein as follows:

One strand each ecru + 524, and 522 (2 strands together) in the first row.

Change to one strand for the next rows. Blend in 522 and 860 into the next row.

Blend in 3860 and 779 for the shadows towards the base.

Fill the right side from dark to light as follows:

One strand each 3860 + 779, and 3363 + 3860, and 3363 (2 strands together) in the first row.

Change to one strand for the next rows. Blend in 522 and 524 into the next row.

Blend in ecru in the next row.

Stitch the centre vein in split stitch using one strand of 779.

4 Large gold-grey-green leaf at bottom centre

Outline the leaf in split stitch using 2 strands of med gold green 3012.

Fill the top side with long and short stitch shading from light to dark, from the outside in towards the centre vein as follows:

One strand each of 3047 + 3013, and 3013 + 3012 (2 strands together) in the first row.

Change to one strand only in the next rows. Blend in 3012.

Fill the right side from dark to light under the turnover as follows:

One strand each of 3860 + 3011, and 2 strands of 3011 (2 strands together) in the first row.

Change to one strand only in the next rows. Blend in 3012 in the next row.

Blend in 3013 in the next row. Blend in 3047 in the next row.

Turnover: work a line of split stitch in one strand of 779 underneath the turnover. Blend in a few straight stitches into this line in 779 for shadow. Outline the turnover in split stitch using 2 strands of 3743. Pad the turnover with straight stitches as shown. Fill the turnover with slanted satin stitch on top of the padding and split stitch, using one strand of 3047.

Stitch the centre vein in split stitch using one strand of 779.

5 Large blossom

Petal 1 at back left

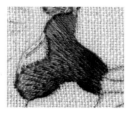

Outline the petal in split stitch using 2 strands of 3042. Start under the turnover and fill with long and short stitch, shading towards the centre base as follows: row 1 = 2 strands 3042; row 2 = 1 strand 3041; row 3 = 1 strand 3740; row 4 = 1 strand 3834; row 5 = 1 strand 154; row 6 = 1 strand 3371.

Turnover: work a line of split stitch in one strand 838 under the turnover. Blend a few straight stitches into this line. Outline the turnover in split stitch using 2 strands 3743 and pad the turnover with straight stitches. Fill the turnover in slanted satin stitch using one strand 3743. Blend a few straight stitches in white over the tip to highlight.

Petal 2 on right

Outline the petal in split stitch using 2 strands 3042. Start at the top edge and shade down towards the centre base with long and short stitch as follows: row 1 = 1 strand each blanc + 3747, and blanc + 3743, and 3042 (2 strands together); row 2 = 1 strand 3042; row 3 = 1 strand 3041; row 4 = 1 strand 3740; row 5 = 1 strand 3834; row 6 = 1 strand 154.

Petal 3 on right

Outline the petal in split stitch using 2 strands 3042. Start at the top edge and shade down towards the centre base with long and short stitch as follows: row 1 = 1 strand each blanc + 3743, and blanc + 3747, and 3042 + 3041 (2 strands together); row 2 = 1 strand each blanc + 3743, and blanc + 3747, and 3042 (2 strands together); row 3 = 1 strand each 3042 + 3041; row 4 = 1 strand each 3041 + 3740; row 5 = 1 strand each 3834 + 154; row 6 = 1 strand 154 + 3371.

Turnover: work a line of split stitch in one strand 838 under the turnover. Blend a few straight stitches into this line. Outline the turnover in split stitch using 2 strands 3743, and pad the turnover with straight stitches. Fill the turnover in slanted satin stitch using one strand 3743.

Petal 4 at bottom

Outline the petal in split stitch using 2 strands 3042. Start at the outside edge under the turnover and shade towards the centre base with long and short stitch, using 2 strands together in the needle as follows: row 1 = 1 strand blanc + 3743, and 3042 + 3041; row 2 = 1 strand 3041 + 3740; change to one strand—row 3 = 1 strand 3834, alternating with 838 and 3371

Turnover: work a line of split stitch in one strand 838 under the turnover. Blend a few straight stitches into this line. Outline the turnover in split stitch using 2 strands 3743, and pad the turnover with straight stitches. Fill the turnover in slanted satin stitch using one strand 3743.

Petal 5

Outline the petal in split stitch using 2 strands 3042. Start at the outside edge and shade towards the centre base with long and short stitch as follows: row 1 = 1 strand blanc + 3743, and 3042 + 3041 (2 strands together); row 2 = 1 strand 3041 alternating with 3740 ; row 3 = 1 strand 3834; row 4 = 1 strand 154.

Turnover: work a line of split stitch in one strand 838 under the turnover. Blend a few straight stitches into this line. Outline the turnover in split stitch using 2 strands 3743 and pad the turnover with straight stitches. Fill the turnover in slanted satin stitch using one strand 3743. Blend in a few straight stitches in white at the tip to highlight.

Blossom centre

Fill the centre with French knots using one strand and 2 loops as follows:
Start at the base and work a few dark knots in one strand each together in the needle 3790 + 780. Change to 782 + 729, then 676 + 677, finally 2 strands 3823.

6 Small white blossoms

Fill each blossom with either one strand Caron Watercolours moonglow or 2 strands DMC blanc. Work straight stitches from the centre out towards the edge of each petal. Fill the centre of each flower with French knots using one strand each 782 + 729 together in the needle.

7 Small buds

Outline each bud in split stitch using one strand 3823. Pad each bud with straight stitches using one strand 3823. Fill each bud with long and short stitch as follows: row 1 = 1 strand 3823; row 2 = blend in 676, then 729.

Blend in a few straight stitches along the base and sides in 3790 to create a shadow.

Work the stems in split stitch using one strand 779.

8 Lavender stalks

Work the stems in split stitch using one strand 3363. Fill each stalk with a bullion knot using about 7 twists in 2 strands Gloriana silk 153 (you can use different shades of plum for each strand in DMC cotton instead).

9 Small green leaves

Fill each leaf with fly stitch using a combination of one strand 3013 + 3011 together in the needle. Work a split stitch line in one strand 779.

BEGINNER LEVEL

The next six projects are simple to follow, with the instructions for long and short

stitch listing the colours needed row by row. I have included alternatives for the

more exotic space dyed and variegated threads.

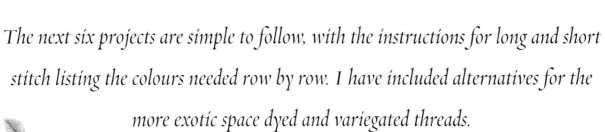

PROJECT 2: PEACH ROSE SPRAY

This project is stitched on off-white linen union fabric.

THREAD KEY

Appleton crewel wool (AP)

pastel peach	877
flesh	707
light flamingo	621
light bright terracotta	222
med bright terracotta	224
dark paprika	725
light peacock blue	641
light autumn yellow	471

Paterna Persian wool (P)   (alternatives Appleton 1 strand)

light khaki green	645	(Appleton 351)
med khaki green	644	(Appleton 342)
dark khaki green	643	(Appleton 344)
very dark khaki green	642	(Appleton 334)
med olive green	653	(Appleton 336)

DMC Cotton (D)

med peach	761

Caron Waterlilies silk (CS)   (alternatives DMC 1 strand)

evergreen	121	(DMC 502)
spruce	107	(DMC 3809 + 502)
kelp	139	(DMC 3012)
cherry	101	(DMC 3722)

Caron Watercolours cotton (CW)   (alternatives)

lime ice	167	(DMC 747 + 3865)
St Tropez	214	(DMC 3809 + 3766)

Chameleon Threads perle No 8 (CA)   (alternative)

lavender	44	(DMC 340 + 210)

Tracing outline

Stitch direction diagram

1 Large rose (split stitch, long and short stitch, satin stitch) AP 222, 224, 621, 707, 725, 877

2 Large leaves (split stitch, long and short stitch) P 642, 643, 644, 645, 653

3 Medium leaves (fly stitch) AP 641; CS 121

4 Small leaves in wool (fly stitch, split stitch) CS 139; AP 641

5 Small clusters of leaves (fly stitch, split stitch) CS 139, CS 107

6 Rosebuds (granitos, straight, fly stitch, split stitch) AP 224, 621, 641, 877; CS 139

7 Apple blossoms (granitos, straight stitch, fly stitch, French knots) AP 471, 877; D 761; CS 101, 107; P 644

8 Lavender spray (bullions, split stitch) CS 139; CA 44

9 Forget-me-nots (French knots) CW 214; AP 725

10 White sprays (split stitch, French knots) CW 167; CS 139

11 Small white flowers (lazy daisy stitch, straight stitch, French knots) CS 139; CW 167

METHOD

Copy the design onto the fabric by your preferred method from the tracing outline.

1 Large rose in centre

Outline the *outer petals* in split stitch using one strand of AP 707.

Fill with long and short stitch, shading from light to dark using one strand each of 5 shades of peach (you will have to mix 2 shades of colour in a row sometimes) as follows: row 1 = 877, 707; row 2 = 621; row 3 = 222, 224.

Fill the centre with satin stitch using one strand 725. Work the two larger middle sections in long and short stitch shading, using one strand as follows: row 1 = 877; row 2 = 707; row 3 = 621.

Fill five smaller sections with satin stitch using one strand as follows from left to right: 621, 707, 877, 621, 877.

2 Large leaves

Outline the leaves with one strand split stitch in P 644. Fill either side of the leaves with long and short stitch, using one strand and shading as follows:

Light side: row 1 = 645; row 2 = 644; row 3 = 643, 642.

Dark side: row 1 = 653; row 2 = 642, 643; row 3 = 644.

Work the centre vein in split stitch in 642.

3 Medium leaves

Use 1 strand of AP 641 and 2 strands of CS 121 together in the needle and fill the shape with fly stitch.

4 Small leaves in wool

Work the stems in split stitch in 2 strands CS 139. Work the leaves in fly stitch in one strand wool AP 641.

5 Small clusters of leaves

Work the stems in split stitch in 2 strands CS 139 and the leaves in fly stitch in 3 strands CS 107.

6 Rosebuds

Work bud in one strand of AP 224 and overlapping petals in AP 877, 621. Work leaves and straight stitches in one strand of AP 641 and CS 139.

7 Apple blossoms

Work petals in straight stitches or granitos using one strand AP 877, tips in one strand D 761. Centre combine one strand each of D 761 and CS 101. French knots: combine one strand each of AP 471 and CS 101. Fill leaves in 2-strand fly stitch using one strand P 644 and one strand CS 107.

8 Lavender spray

Stitch using 2 strands CS 139 for split stitch stems and 2 strands CA 44 for bullions.

9 Forget-me-nots

Fill with French knots using one strand CW 214 and centre in AP 725.

10 White sprays

Work stems in split stitch using 2 strands CS 139 and flowers in French knots using one strand CW 167.

11 Small white flowers

Work petals in lazy daisy stitches using one strand CW 167, and centre in French knots using 2 strands CS 139.

PROJECT 3: PLUM, PINK AND OFF-WHITE ROSE SPRAY

This project is stitched on off-white Belgian linen.

THREAD KEY

Appleton crewel wool (AP)

cream	992
pale dull rose pink	141
light dull rose pink	142
light wine red	712
light chocolate brown	183
custard yellow	851
light grey green	352
light Jacobean green	292
med Jacobean green	293
dark Jacobean green	294
very dark drab green	336

DMC rayon (R) (alternative)

gold	30676	(DMC cotton 728)

DMC stranded cotton (D)

light rose	152

DMC metallic (M)

gold	5282

Caron Watercolours cotton (CW) (alternatives 2 strands cotton or mix)

vanilla	098	(DMC cotton 3865)
desert sage	033	(DMC cotton mix 501+3861)

Caron Waterlilies silk (CS) (alternative 1 strand cotton)

antique rose	108	(DMC cotton 3835)

Gumnut Buds perle (G) (alternatives 2 strands)

eucalypt	624	(DMC cotton 3052)
khaki	645	(DMC cotton 3012)

Tracing outline

Stitch direction diagram

1 Large leaves (split stitch, long and short stitch) AP 292, 293, 294, 336, 352; M 5282

2 Smaller leaves (fly stitch) CW 033

3 Main rose (split stitch, long and short stitch, satin stitch) AP 141, 142, 183, 712, 992

4 Veins (split stitch) G 624

5 Apple blossoms (granitos, French knots, lazy daisy stitch, straight stitch) CW 033, 098; AP 851; R 30676; D 152; CS 108

6 Rosebuds (granitos, fly stitch, straight stitch) AP 142, 352, 712, 992; G 645; M 5282

7 Small daisies (lazy daisy stitch, French knots) CS 108; R 30676; AP 851; G 645

8 Lavender sprays (bullion knots) CS 108

9 Forget-me-nots (French knots, lazy daisy stitch) AP 712, D 152, G 645, CW 098, R 30676

10 Leaf sprays (lazy daisy stitch) G 645

METHOD

Copy the design onto the fabric by your preferred method from the tracing outline.

1 Large leaves

Outline each leaf with split stitch using one strand AP 292. Fill on either side of each leaf from the outside in towards the centre vein in long and short stitch shading, using one strand AP as follows:

Light side: row 1 = 352, 292; row 2 = 293.
Dark side: row 1 = 336; row 2 = 294.

Work the smaller leaves as follows:

Light side: row 1 = 352; row 2 = 292.
Dark side: row 1 = 336; row 2 = 294.

Work the centre vein in split stitch in gold.

2 Smaller leaves

Fill each leaf in fly stitch using one strand CW 033.

3 Main rose

Start with the petals. Outline each petal with split stitch using one strand AP 141 and fill with long and short stitch shading using one strand wool, from the outside edge in as follows:

Large petals: row 1 = 992; row 2 = 141; row 3 = 142; row 4 = 183. Work a few straight stitches in 183 in the centre.

Smaller petals: row 1 = 992; row 2 = 142, 183. Work the inner sections of the centre petal next. Using one strand 712 fill the inner section with satin stitch and the lip with satin stitch in 712. Work a line of split stitch in 183. Stitch the centre petal with split stitch in 992.

4 Veins for lavender and leaves

Work all the veins in split stitch using one strand G 624.

5 Apple blossoms

Work each petal in one strand CW 098. For the straight stitches in the centre use a blend of one strand each D 152 + CS 108. Use a blend of one strand each AP 851 + R 30676 for the French knots in the centre. Work the leaves in lazy daisy stitches in one strand CW 033.

6 Rosebuds

Fill bud in either granitos or straight stitch in one strand AP 712. Work side petals in straight stitches using one strand AP 142 and overlap second petal in AP 992. Make a few straight stitches from base to centre bud using one strand AP 352. Make a large fly stitch on sides and secure at base in one strand G 645. Add a fly stitch and a straight stitch at the top of the bud and over the base of bud in one strand M 5282.

7 Small daisy flowers

Work lazy daisy stitches around the centre using one strand CS 108 (or 2 strands cotton). Fill centre with French knots using a combination of one strand each AP 851 + R 30676. Work lazy daisy stitches for leaves using one strand G 645.

8 Lavender sprays

Work two bullions next to each other for each bud, using 2 strands CS 108.

9 Forget-me-nots

Work in French knots using a combination of one strand each AP 712 + D 152 for plum flowers and CW 098 + R 30676 for white flowers. Work leaves in lazy daisy stitch using one strand G 645. Scatter a few knots in white through the leaves and flowers as shown.

10 Leaf sprays

Work the sprays in lazy daisy stitches using one strand G 645.

PROJECT 4: CREAM ROSE SPRAY ON YELLOW FABRIC

This project is stitched on a yellow furnishing weight cotton fabric.

THREAD KEY

Appleton crewel wool (AP)

pastel cream	871
pale heraldic gold	841
light honeysuckle yellow	692
light drab fawn	952
med chocolate	184

med honeysuckle yellow	693
light drab green	331
light olive	241
med mid olive	344
dark mid olive	346
very dark mid olive	347

Caron Watercolours cotton (CW)

(alternatives 2 strands cotton or mix)

sierra	222	(DMC 520 + 522)
lavender mist	004	(DMC 3747 + 156)
pearl	078	(DMC 3865)

Caron Waterlilies silk (CS)

(alternatives 1 strand cotton or mix)

kelp	139	(DMC 975 + 3012)
moonglow	146	(DMC 3747)

ABBREVIATION KEY

1. Large leaves (split stitch, long and short stitch)
   AP 241, 331, 344, 346, 347
2. Large rose (split stitch, long and short stitch)
   AP 184, 692, 841, 871, 952
3. Small leaves (fly stitch) CW 222
4. White flower (straight stitch, French knots)
   CW 078; CS 139; AP 693
5. Blue daisies (lazy daisy stitch, French knots)
   CW 004; CS 139; AP 693
6. Rosebuds (granitos, straight stitch, fly stitch)
   AP 241, 692, 693, 841, 871; CS 139
7. Stems (split stitch) CS 139
8. Lavender (bullion) CS 146
9. French knot flowers (French knots) CW 004
10. Very small leaves (lazy daisy stitch) CS 139

Stitch direction diagram

Tracing outline

METHOD

Copy the design onto the fabric by your preferred method from the tracing outline.

1 Large leaves

Do not outline the leaves with split stitch. Fill each side of the leaf with long and short stitch in AP, using one strand and shading as follows:

Light side: row 1 = 331; row 2 = 241; row 3 = 344.

Dark side: row 1 = 347; row 2 = 346; row 3 = 344.

Fill the centre vein in split stitch using one strand of 347.

2 Large rose

Start with the three large petals at base and mid left.

Outline each petal in split stitch before filling with long and short stitch, using one strand AP, from the outside edge in as follows: row 1 = 871; row 2 = 841, 692; row 3 = 952. Add a few straight stitches in 184.

Two medium petals: row 1 = 871; row 2 = 692; row 3 = 952.

Small petal at top: row 1 = 692; row 2 = 952. Fill the inner centre with adjacent rows of split stitch in the 2 darkest shades of brown. Fill the next inner section with adjacent rows of split stitch in the 2 darkest shades of cream. Fill the outside section with adjacent rows of split stitch in the lightest shade of cream.

3 Small leaves

Cut off a piece of thread that shades from green to gold tan. Fill each leaf with fly stitch using two strands CW 222.

4 White flowers

Fill petals with straight stitches in one strand CW 078. Work a few small straight stitches near the centre of the petals in one strand CS 139. In the centre work French knots with 2 strands CS 139 + one strand AP 693 together in the needle.

5 Blue daisy flowers

Work lazy daisy stitches for the petals using one strand CW 004. Work the centre in French knots using 2 strands CS 139 + 1 strand AP 693 together in the needle.

6 Rosebuds

Two small rosebuds: work centre in straight stitch or granitos using one strand AP 692 and outer petals in one strand AP 871.

Three large rosebuds: fill the bud with straight stitches using one strand AP 693 and the outer petals using one strand AP 871 and 841.

Embroider straight stitches over the base of the buds for the sepals using one strand AP 241 and some in CS 139. Work a small fly stitch at the tip using one strand of CS 139 then add one straight stitch. Add lazy daisy stitches at the base for leaves, using one strand of AP 241 and a small straight stitch inside this.

7 Stems

Work all stems in 2 lines of split stitch in CS 139.

8 Lavender spray

Make 2 bullion stitches side by side using 2 strands CS 146.

9 French knot flowers

Scatter French knots around the stem and branches using one strand CW 004.

10 Very small leaves

Work all the little leaves using a lazy daisy stitch with a straight stitch in the centre using one strand CS 139.

PROJECT 5: ORANGE POPPY AND RIBBON

This project is stitched on DMC natural 32 count linen with an iron-on interfacing to stabilise the fabric.

THREAD KEY

DMC stranded cotton (D)

pale yellow	744
light yellow	743
med yellow	742
light orange	741
med orange	721
dark orange	920
rust red	355
off white	3865
cream	746
dark cream	3823
pale yellow	745
light custard yellow	3855
med custard yellow	3854
dark custard yellow	3853
rust	301
dark rust	400
very dark rust	300
med plum brown	3861
dark plum brown	779
dark brown	838
very dark brown	3371

Cascade House shaded crewel wool (CA)
(alternatives Appleton 1 strand)

pale green	7280/2	(AP pale grey green 352)
light green	7280/4	(AP light grey green 353)
med green	7280/6	(AP med grey green 354)
dark green	7280/10	(AP dark grey green 355/6)

DMC metallic (M)

copper	E301

Gloriana silk (GS)   (alternative cotton 1 strand)

seaweed	088	(DMC 935)

Gumnut Buds perle (GB)   (alternative cotton 2 strands)

dark jacaranda	287	(DMC 3746)

Tracing outline

ABBREVIATION KEY

1 Ribbon (long and short stitch) D 355, 721, 741, 742, 743, 744, 920

2 Leaves (split stitch, long and short stitch) CA 7280 2, 7280 4, 7280 6, 7280 10; M E301

3 Poppy (split stitch, long and short, straight stitch) D 300, 301, 400, 745, 746, 3823, 3853, 3854, 3855, 3865

4 Poppy centre (French knots, straight stitch) D 779, 838, 3371, 3861

5 Small leaves (split stitch, straight stitch) GS 088

6 Small blossoms (lazy daisy stitch, French knots, straight stitch) GB 287; D 301, 3823, 3854

7 French knot blossoms (French knots) D 3823

METHOD

Copy the design onto the fabric by your preferred method from the tracing outline.

1 Ribbon

Fill the ribbon with long and short stitch in D. Work the underneath area first, blending the shades as follows: row 1 = 355; row 2 = 920; row 3 = 721; row 4 = 741; row 5 = 742.

Work the top lighter areas as follows: row 1 = 744; row 2 = 743; row 3 = 742; row 4 = 741; row 5 = 721; row 6 = 920; row 7 = 355.

2 Leaves

Outline each leaf with split stitch using one strand CA 7280 6. Fill each side of the leaf with long and short stitch, starting from the outside edge in towards the centre vein, using one strand.

Work the two large leaves at left and below as follows:

Light side: row 1 = 7280 2; row 2 = 7280 4; row 3 = 7280 6. Blend in a few straight stitches in 7280 10 to accent shadows.

Stitch direction diagram

Dark side: row 1 = 7280 10; row 2 = 7280 6; row 3 = 7280 4. Blend in a few straight stitches in 7280 2 to accent highlights.

Work the leaf at top as follows:

Left side: row 1 = 7280 4; row 2 = 7280 6; row 3 = 7280 10.

Right side: row 2 = 7280 10; row 2 = 7280 6.

Work the two small leaves on right as follows:

Larger leaf, light side: row 1 = 7280 2; row 2 = 7280 4; darker side: row 1 = 7280 10; row 2 = 7280 6.

Smaller leaf, light side: satin stitch in 7280 2; dark side: satin stitch in 7280 6.

Work the centre vein in split stitch using one strand M E301.

3 Poppy

Start with the back petals and work forward. Outline each petal with one strand of split stitch in D 3854 as you work. Fill each petal with long and short stitch from the outside edge in towards the centre, using 2 strands in the first row and one strand for each subsequent row as follows:

Petal one, top right: row 1 = 3855, 3854, 3853; row 2 = 3853, 400.

Petal two, bottom right: row 1 = 3854, 3853, 301; row 2 = 301, 400.

Petal three, top right: row 1 = 745, 3853, 3854; row 2 = 3853; row 3 = 301, 400; row 4 = 300.

Petal four, large centre right: row 1 = 3865, 746, 3823; row 2 = 3823, 745; row 3 = 3855, 3854; row 4 = 3853, 301; row 5 = 400.

Petal five, small on top left: row 1 = 745, 3855; row 2 = 3854; row 3 = 3853, 400.

Petal six, bottom half of large on left: row 1 = 746, 3823; row 2 = 3855, 3854; row 3 = 3853.

Petal seven, top half of large on left: row 1 = 746, 3823, 3855; row 2 = 3823, 745, 3855, 3854; row 3 = 3855, 3854, 3853; row 4 = 3853, 301; row 5 = 301, 400.

Petal eight, small dark bit behind front petal: row 1 = 3853, 301; row 2 = 400, 300.

Petal nine, large petal top centre: row 1 = 3865, 746, 3823, 745; row 2 = 746, 3823, 745, 3855; row 3 = 745, 3855, 3854, 3853; row 4 = 3855, 3854, 3853; row 5 = 3853, 301; row 6 = 301, 400; row 6 = 400.

Petal ten, middle petal under centre: row 1 = 746, 3823; row 2 = 745, 3855; row 3 = 3854.

4 Poppy centre

Start at the bottom and work up. Using 2 strands, fill the centre with French knots shading from dark to light in D 838, 779, 3861. Using one strand 3371, make straight lines from the centre out over the petals. Using one strand each 3861 + 3371 together in the needle, scatter loose French knots among the straight lines.

5 Small leaves and stems

Work the leaves in one strand of split stitch. Outline each leaf with split stitch in GS 088, using one strand, and fill with straight stitches.

6 Small blossoms

Fill around the centre with lazy daisy stitches using one strand GB 287 (or 2 strands cotton). Make straight stitches on the centre of each lazy daisy stitch in D 3823. Work French knots using a combination of one strand each 3854 + 301 together in the needle.

7 French knot flowers

Scatter French knots among the blossoms as shown using one strand GB 287 or 2 strands D 3823.

PROJECT 6: DAISY AND PINK RIBBON SPRAY

This project is stitched on off-white Belgian linen.

THREAD KEY

Gumnut Daisies wool (GW)		(alternative Appleton 1 strand)
pale green	641	(331A)
light green	643	(331)
med green	645	(332)
dark green	646	(334)
very dark green	648	(336)
cream	742	(841)
light yellow	743	(842)

med pink	865	(754)
light pink	850	(751)
off white	991	(991)
pale blue	344	(741)

Gumnut Buds perle (GP)		(alternative DMC 2 strands)
pale yellow	742	(3823)
light yellow	743	(3822)
deep plum	179	(3685)

Tracing outline

dark blue grey	998	(3750)
brown	967	(3860)
med yellow	744	(3821)
dark yellow	746	(3820)
gold	947	(434)
dark gold	949	(433)
white	990	(blanc)

Gumnut Stars silk (GS) **(alternative DMC 1 strand)**

med khaki green	645	(3012)
dark khaki green	648	(3011)
dark gold	947	(434)

DMC stranded cotton (D)

dark green	934
off white	712
pale pink	225

light pink	152
med pink	223
plum brown	3861
dark plum brown	3860
very dark plum brown	779
very dark brown	3371

DMC metallic (M)

| antique silver | E677 |

Stitch direction diagram

ABBREVIATION KEY

1 Ribbon (split, long and short stitch) D 152, 223, 225, 712, 779, 3860

2 Large leaves (split stitch, long and short stitch) GW 641, 643, 645, 646, 648; D 934; M E677

3 Daisy (split stitch, long and short, straight stitch) GW 742, 743, 991; D 3860, 3861

4 Daisy centre (French knots) GP 742, 743, 744, 746, 947, 949, 990; D 3371

5 Rosebuds (padded satin stitch, split stitch, straight stitch, fly stitch) GW 850, 865, 991; GS 645, 648; M E677

6 Wheat (bullions, split stitch, straight stitch) GP 742, 743; GS 947

7 Gypsophila (French knots) GP 179, 998

8 Blue spray (straight stitch, French knots) GW 344; GS 645, 648

9 Small leaves (fly stitch) GP 967

10 Stems (split stitch) GS 648

METHOD

Copy the design onto the fabric by your preferred method from the tracing outline.

1 Ribbon

Outline each section with split stitch using 2 strands D 152. Fill each section of the ribbon with long and short stitch using 2 strands in the first row and one strand thereafter as follows:

Short end: row 1 = 779; row 2 = 3860; row 3 = 223; row 4 = 152; row 5 = 225

Front loop, inner: underneath: row 1 = 779; row 2 = 3860; row 3 = 223; row 4 = 152; row 5 = 3860; row 6 = 779

Front loop, outer: top: row 1 = 223; row 2 = 152; row 3 = 225; row 5 = 712; row 6 = 225; row 7 = 152; row 8 = 223; row 9 = 3860; row 10 = 779

Top loop, inner: row 1 = 779; row 2 = 3860; row 3 = 223; row 4 = 3860; row 5 = 779

Top loop, outer: row 1 = 712; row 2 = 225; row 3 = 152; row 4 = 223; row 5 = 3860; row 6 = 779

2 Large leaves

Outline each leaf with split stitch using one strand GW 643. Leave the centre vein free. Fill on either side of each leaf in long and short stitch using one strand wool as follows:

Back leaf (right): top side: row 1 = 641, 643, 645; row 2 = 643, 645, 646; row 3 = 646, 648

Bottom side: row 1 = 643, 645, 646; row 2 = 645, 646, 648; row 3 = 646, 648

Centre leaf: top side: row 1 = 643, 645, 646; row 2 = 645, 646, 648

Bottom side: row 1 = 641, 643, 645; row2 = 643, 645; row 3 = 645, 646; row 4 = 646, 648

Leaf on left: top side: row 1 = 641, 643; row 2 = 643, 645; row 3 = 645

Bottom side: row 1 = 648; row 2 = 646; row 3 = 645, 643; row 4 = 643

Work the centre vein with one strand D 934 in split stitch. Work a second line next to and slightly on top of this in one strand M E677.

3 Daisy

Outline each petal with split stitch using one strand GW 991. Fill each petal with one strand of long and short stitch, starting at the outer edge and working in towards the centre, shading as follows: GW 991, 742, 743. When the petal is complete take one strand D 3861 and work a few straight stitches at the centre and along the side (underside) of the petals to create a shadow. Next take one strand D 3860 and work stitches in between the first ones to deepen the shadow.

4 Daisy centre

Using one strand of perle, fill the centre with French knots shading from dark to light from base to top as follows: GP 949, 947, 746, 744, 743, 742, 990. Scatter loose French knots around the base and a few on the top in one strand D 3371.

5 Rosebuds

Outline the bud centre with split stitch in one strand GW 865. Fill with padded satin stitch in GW 865, working from base to tip. Take one strand GW 850 and work straight stitches from the base over to the right side of the bud. Take one strand GW 991 and work a second petal from the base over to the left side of the bud. Add straight stitches over the base of the bud in one strand GS 645 and 648. Take one strand M E677 and work a few straight stitches in between these. Fill the calyx and leaves with satin stitch in GS 645. Work a small fly stitch at the tip of the bud in one strand GS 645 and another close to this in one strand M E677.

6 Wheat

Work the centre vein in split stitch using one strand GS 947. Work a bullion on each grain using one strand GP 742 and about 6 twists. Work a second

bullion close to this using one strand GP 743 and about 7 twists. Work a straight stitch down the centre of both bullions using 2 strands GS 947. Make straight stitches from the end of the bullions out for the whiskers, using one strand GS 947.

7 Gypsophila

Scatter French knots randomly around the stalks and stem using one strand GP 179 and 998.

8 Blue spray

Work the stems and stalks in split stitch using one strand GS 648. Fill each bud with straight stitches from the base out towards the tip using one strand GW 344. Work a few tiny straight stitches at the base of each in one strand GS 645, and a French knot with one strand GS 645.

9 Small leaves

Fill each leaf in fly stitch using one strand GP 967.

10 Stems

Work all stems in split stitch using one strand GS 648.

PROJECT 7: DAISY AND BLUE RIBBON SPRAY

This project is stitched on off-white Belgian linen.

THREAD KEY

DMC stranded cotton (D)

pale lavender	3747
light grey blue	159
med grey blue	160
dark grey blue	161
dark grey	413
very dark grey	3799
very dark brown	3371
light plum	3042
medium plum	3041
light gold	3047
light khaki gold	372
med khaki gold	370
dark khaki green	3011
very dark khaki green	936
light blue grey	415
med blue grey	318
light brown grey	648
med brown grey	647
dark brown grey	645
cream	746
pale yellow	745
light golden brown	612
med brown	3790
dark brown	3781
light mauve	3836
med mauve	3835
dark mauve	3834
light mauve pink	3727

Cascade House shaded crewel wool (CA)
(alternative 1 strand Appleton)

white	1000/2	(AP 991)

Gumnut Buds perle (GP) (alternatives 2 strands DMC)

med khaki	645	(D 3012)

Tracing outline

ABBREVIATION KEY

1 Ribbon (long and short stitch, split stitch) D 159, 160, 161, 413, 3041, 3042, 3371, 3747, 3799

2 Large and small leaves (long and short stitch, split) D 370, 372, 936, 3011, 3047, 3781

3 Daisy (long and short stitch, straight stitch) D 160, 318, 415, 645, 647, 648, 3042, 3047; CA 1000 2

4 Daisy centre (French knots) D 612, 745, 746, 3047, 3371, 3781, 3790, 3834

5 Small leaves (fly stitch) GP 645

6 Stems (split stitch) D 3011

7 Lavender (bullions) D 3834, 3835, 3836

8 Forget-me-nots (French knots) D 745, 3727

Stitch direction diagram

Copy the design onto the fabric by your preferred method from the tracing outline.

1 Ribbon

Outline all the ribbon segments in split stitch and fill with long and short stitch using one strand DMC as follows:

Top right tail: row 1 = 3747, 159; row 2 = 159, 160; row 3 = 161; row 4 = 413 ; row 5 = 3799, 3371.

Top right loop, underneath: row 1 = 161; row 2 = 413; row 3 = 3799; row 4 = 3371.

Bottom left tail: row 1 = 159; row 2 = 160; row 3 = 161; row 4 = 413; row 5 = 3799; row 6 = 3371.

Bottom left, section near leaf: row 1 = 160; row 2 = 161; row 3 = 413; row 4 = 3799; row 5 = 3371.

Lower loop, reverse: row 1 = 3799, 3371; row 2 = 413; row 3 = 161; row 4 = 160; row 5 = 413; row 6 = 3799, 3371.

Lower loop, front: row 1 = 3747; row 2 = 159; row 3 = 160; row 4 = 161; row 5 = 413; row 6 = 3799; row 7 = 3371.

Blend in a few straight stitches using one strand 3042 and 3041 as highlights (optional).

2 Large and small leaves

Outline all the large leaves in split stitch leaving the centre vein free. Fill the leaves with long and short stitch using 2 strands DMC in the first row and one strand thereafter as follows:

Smaller leaf, top right: top dark side: row 1 = 3011; row 2 = 936.

Light side: row 1 = 3011, 370; row 2 = 372; row 3 = 3047.

Larger leaf lower right, dark side: row 1 = 936 + 3011; row 2 = 3011; row 3 = 370; row 4 = 372; row 5 = 3047.

Light side: row 1 = 3047, 372; row 2 = 372, 370; row 3 = 370.

Large leaf at left: same as large leaf on right.

NB Underline edges under petals with one line of split stitch in D 936 before stitching petals.

Small leaf upper left: light side: row 1 = 3047, 372; dark side: row 1 = 3011; row 2 = 370.

Small leaf upper right: light side: row 1 = 3047; row 2 = 372; dark side: row 1 = 370; row 2 = 3011.

Stitch the centre veins in split stitch using one strand 3781.

3 Daisy

Outline each petal with split stitch using one strand CA 1000 2. Fill each petal with long and short stitch using one strand CA 1000 2, leaving a small space between the overlaps of each petal. On top of the wool blend in straight stitches, at the tips and base of each petal, using one strand DMC as follows:

Blue-grey petals: tip 160, 318, 415; base: 648, 647, 645.

Mauve-grey petals: tip: 160, 3042, 415; base: 648, 647, 645. Blend in 3042 and 645 for shadows on inner edges (underneath) of petals.

On the front petals blend in a few straight stitches in one strand D 3047 to highlight.

4 Daisy centre

Fill the centre with French knots using 2 strands DMC and shading as follows:

From base to top: row 1 = 3790, 3781, 3834; row 2 = 612; row 3 = 3047; row 4 = 746, 745. Use the photo as a guide to placing the shades.

Around the edge scatter loose French knots using one strand of D 3371. Scatter a few knots in 612 among these.

5 Small leaves

Fill the leaves in fly stitch in one strand GP 645.

6 Stems and grasses

Work all the stems and grasses in split stitch in 2 strands D 3011.

7 Lavender spray

Fill each bud with 2 adjacent bullions using 7 wraps for each and 2 strands D 3836, 3835, 3834. Use the darker shades at the top, going lighter at the bottom.

8 Forget-me-nots

Fill each flower with French knots, using 2 strands D 3727, with some in D 745.

INTERMEDIATE LEVEL

The next five projects are more suited to the embroiderer who has a little previous experience of long and short stitch embroidery and some understanding of placing the listed colours. You may find it helpful to use the photos as a guide.

PROJECT 8: JANEY'S POPPY WITH DAISY SPRAY

This project is stitched on DMC natural 32 count linen with a medium iron-on interfacing to stabilise the fabric.

THREAD KEY

DMC (D) and Anchor (A) stranded cotton

pale grey green	D 3024 + A 213
light grey green	D 3023 + A 858
med grey green	D 3022 + A 859
dark grey green	D 645 + A 860
very dark grey	D 3787
pale gold green	A 842
light gold green	D 3013
med gold green	D 3012
dark gold green	D 830

metallic gold	D 5282
pale lilac	D 3743
pale lime green	D 165
dark fuchsia pink	D 3803
light coffee brown	D 3863

Gloriana silk (GS)

ollalieberry	153
light pink valentine	036
med pink rose flame	070
dark pink pomegranate	139

lavender twilight	089
vanilla	003
green olive grove	116

Gloriana Lorikeet crewel wool (GW)

white fresh snow	102W3
peach blush	098W3
pomegranate pastel	139W1
gold green Spanish moss	048W

Tracing outline

ABBREVIATION KEY

1 Large grey-green leaves (split stitch, long and short stitch, straight) D 3024 + A 213, D 3023 + A 858, D 3022 + A 859, D 645 + A 860; D 3787, 5282; GS 153

2 Large gold-green leaves (split stitch, long and short stitch, straight stitch) A 842; D 830, 3012, 3013, 3787, 5282

3 Poppy (split stitch, long and short stitch, straight stitch) D 165, 3012, 3743, 3787, 3803; GS 003, 036, 070, 089, 139

4 Daisies (split stitch, long and short stitch, straight stitch, French knot) D 165, 830, 3863; GW 102W3, 098W3, 139W1

5 Lavender (split stitch, long and short stitch, French knot) GS 089, 116, 153; D 830

6 White flower sprays (split stitch, French knots) D 830; GS 003

7 Dark pink blossoms (satin stitch, French knots, straight stitch, fly stitch) D 165, 830; GS 116, 139

8 Light green leaves (fly stitch) GW 048

9 Buds (long and short stitch, straight stitch) GW 098W3, 102W3, 139W1; D 3863

10 Small leaves (fly stitch) GS 116

11 Stems (split stitch) D 830

METHOD

Copy the design onto the fabric by your preferred method from the tracing outline.

1 Large grey-green leaves

Outline each leaf with split stitch, leaving the centre vein free, using 2 strands D 3023. Fill either side of the leaf with long and short stitch using 2 strands: D 3024 + A 213, D 3023 + A 858, D 3022 + A 859 , D 645 + A 860, D 3787 (one each of the blends in the needle). Shade from the outside in towards the centre vein, from light to dark or dark to light. Using one strand GS 153 blend in a few straight stitches as shown in the photo. Work the centre vein in split stitch in one strand D 5282.

2 Large gold-green leaves

Outline each leaf with split stitch leaving the centre vein free, using 2 strands D 3013. Fill either side of the leaf with long and short stitch, using 2 strands A 842, D 3013, 3012, 830, 3787. Shade from the outside in towards the centre vein, from light to dark or dark to light. Using one strand 3787, blend in a few straight stitches to add shadow. Work the centre vein in split stitch in one strand 5282.

Stitch direction diagram

3 Poppy

Start with the back petals and work forward. Outline each petal in split stitch in 2 strands GS 070. Working from the outside in towards the centre, fill each petal with long and short stitch, using GS 036, 070, 139. Change to one strand GS 089 and then D 3743 in the centre. Emphasise the shadows under each petal with one strand D 3803 in split stitch and work a few straight stitches into the existing shading. Work the turnovers in padded satin stitch using one strand GS 036.

Work the lower centre section in satin stitch in one strand D 3012 and the upper section in D 165, working the stitches from the centre point out towards the edges. Work a French knot in the centre in D 3012 and then make a few straight stitches out from this knot to the edge in one strand D 3787 (this is the shadow under the vanilla straight stitch). Close to these make random straight stitches in GS 003. Continue to make these random stitches around the lavender area as shown in the photo.

4 Daisies

Outline each daisy petal with one strand GW 102W3. Starting with the back petals, fill each one with long and short stitch using one strand GW 102W3, 139W1, 098W3, and finally work a few straight stitches in one strand D 3863. Work the centre in French knots using one strand each D 830 + 165 together in the needle. Work the stem in split stitch using one strand each 830 and 165.

5 Lavender stalks

Work the stems with split stitch in one strand D 830. Fill each leaf with long and short stitch using 2 strands GS 116. Work the lavender flower in French knots using one strand each GS 089 + 153 together in the needle.

6 White flower sprays

Work the stems in split stitch in D 830. Work the flowers in French knots using 2 strands GS 003.

7 Dark pink blossoms

Work each petal in satin stitch using 2 strands GS 139. Work the centre in French knots using one strand each D 830 + 165 together in the needle. Work small straight stitches between the petals in one strand D 165. Work the leaves in fly stitch using 2 strands GS 116.

8 Light green leaves

Fill each leaf with fly stitch using one strand GW 048.

9 Buds

Work the buds by outlining each segment with split stitch in one strand GW 102W3 and filling in with long and short stitch shading using one strand each GW 102W3, 139W1, 098W3; ensure that the centre bud is in the darkest shade. Use one strand D 3863 to add straight stitches in the centres.

10 Small leaves

Fill each leaf with fly stitch using 2 strands GS 116.

11 Stems

Work each stem in split stitch using one strand D 830.

PROJECT 9: PALE CREAM AND PINK ROSE SPRAY

This project is stitched on off-white linen union with a medium iron-on interfacing to stabilise the fabric.

THREAD KEY

Gloriana Lorikeet crewel wool (GW)

fresh snow	102W3
vanilla	003W3
Arctic ice pastel	138W1
Arctic ice light	138W2
Arctic ice	138W3

Gloriana silk (GS)

winter woods	010
antique gold	086
rosebud pink	137b
sandstone rose	141
desert rose	106
pigeon	140
ollalieberry	153
slate green	051

DMC stranded cotton (D)

pale gold	3047
light gold	372
med gold	371
dark green gold	3011
dark grey	535

Tracing outline

ABBREVIATION KEY

1 Large grey-green leaves (split stitch, long and short stitch, straight stitch) GW 138W1, 138W2, 138W3; GS 051, 153; D 3047

2 Large gold leaf and sepals (split stitch, long and short stitch, straight stitch) GS 010; D 371, 372, 3011, 3047

3 Rose (split stitch, long and short stitch, straight stitch) GW 003W3, 102W3; GS 106, 137b, 140, 141, 153; D 535

4 Rosebuds (split stitch, long and short stitch) GS 010, 106, 137b, 141, 153; D 371, 3011, 3047

5 Pink blossoms (split stitch, long and short stitch, straight stitch) GS 106, 051, 137b, 141; GW 138W2, 138W3

6 Yellow blossoms (split stitch, long and short stitch, straight stitch, French knots) GW 003W3; GS 010, 086; D 372

7 Small grey-green leaves (fly stitch) GW 138W1, 138W2, 138W3

8 Small gold leaves (fly stitch) D 372, 371, 3011, 3047; GS 010

9 Small mauve flowers (French knots) GS 153; D 3047

10 Stems (split stitch) D 371, 3011

11 Strokes (stem stitch, satin stitch) D 140, 141, 153

METHOD
Copy the design onto the fabric by your preferred method from the tracing outline.

1 Large grey-green leaves

Outline the leaves with split stitch in one strand GW 138W2. Fill on either side of each leaf with long and short stitch using one strand GW 138W1, 138W2, 138W3. Shade from the outside in towards the centre vein in either light to dark or dark to light. Take one strand GS 051 and work split stitch down the centre vein. Take one strand GS 153 and blend in a few straight stitches as shown in the photo. Take one strand D 3047 and blend in a few straight stitches as highlights as shown in the photo

2 Sepals on rose plus large gold leaf

Outline each sepal with one strand D 371. Start with the back sepals and fill each one with long and short stitch using one strand D 3047, 3011, 372, 371, GS 010, from the top down towards the narrow base, shading from light to dark. Take one strand GS 010 and work a few split stitches along one side and beyond to create a fine line along the tip.

Stitch direction diagram

3 Rose

This rose is worked with a foundation of long and short stitch in 2 strands GW 102W3, 003W3, and the shading is added afterwards in straight stitch with silk. Start with the back petals. Outline each one with split stitch using one strand GS 003W3. Fill each petal with long and short stitch, shading from the outside in towards the centre using one strand GW 102W3 and 003W3. Leave the turnovers free. Take one strand each of GS137b, 141, 106, 140 and blend in straight stitches along the bases and under the turnovers to create a shadowed effect. Take one strand D 535 and blend in where the deep shadows are required, using the photo as a guide. Outline the turnovers with one strand GS 102W3 in split stitch, and pad with loose long stitches before working satin stitch at an angle over this. You can work in a few straight stitches at the base of the turnover with 137b on the larger turnovers. Work a line of stem stitch at the base of the rose in GS 153 to add definition.

4 Rosebuds

Outline the buds with split stitch in one strand GS 141. Fill the buds with long and short stitch using one strand GS 141, 106, 153, 137b. Work a few straight stitches at the base in one strand GS 153. To work the sepals, outline each one in split stitch using one strand 371. Fill with long and short stitch, using one strand D 3047, 371, 3011, shading from light to dark towards the base. Take one strand GS 010 and work a few small stitches at the base and some split stitches along the sepal tips. Use the photo as a guide.

5 Pink blossoms

Outline each segment with split stitch using one strand GS 141 and fill with long and short stitch, using one strand GS 137b, 141, 106, 051, shading from light to dark pink. Work the sepals at the base using one strand GS 138W3, then work a few straight stitches on top of this in 138W2.

6 Yellow blossoms

Outline each petal with split stitch using one strand GW 003W3. Fill each petal with satin stitch using one strand 003W3 and blend in one strand each GS 086 and 372 on top of this. Fill the centre with French knots using one strand GS 010.

7 Small grey-green leaves

Fill each leaf with fly stitch, using one strand of either GW 138W1, 138W2 or 138W3.

8 Small gold leaves

Fill each leaf with fly stitch in a different shade of gold: light gold = D 3047 + D 372; med gold = D 372 + D 371; dark gold = GS 010 + D 3011.

9 Small mauve flowers

Fill each flower with French knots using 2 strands GS 153; work the centres in D 3047.

10 Stems

Work all the stems in split stitch using one strand of either D 371 or 3011.

11 Stroke work

Use 2 strands of either D 153, 140 or 141, work each stroke with stem stitch, starting with the darkest shade at the bottom and working forward to the lightest shade. Fill the bulb ends with satin stitch.

Project 10: Red poppy spray

This project is stitched on off-white Belgian linen.

THREAD KEY

Cascade House shaded crewel wool (CA)

pale green	7250/2	med olive green	7280/4
light green	7250/4	dark olive green	7280/6
med green	7250/6	pale lavender	5370/2
dark green	7250/8	light lavender	5370/4
grey	7940/6	med lavender	5370/6
pale olive	1000/10	dark lavender	5370/10
light olive green	7280/2	charcoal	9990/6
		off white	1000/4

Tracing outline

DMC stranded cotton (D)

dark grey	3787	very dark rust red	3857	grey green	3022
pale peach	3770	dark brown	838	pale gold	3047
light peach	353	very dark brown	3371	light gold	3046
med peach	352	off white	3865	medium gold	3045
dark peach	351	pale lilac	3743	dark gold	167
light rust red	3830	light lilac	3042		
med rust red	355	med grey	318	**Gloriana silk (GS)**	
dark rust red	3777	dark grey	317	apricot grove	076
		very dark grey	3799	fall foliage	077

Stitch direction diagram

ABBREVIATION KEY

1 Large grey-green leaves (split stitch, long and short stitch, straight stitch) CA 7250/2, 7250/4, 7250/6, 7250/8, 7940/6; D 3787; GS 077

2 Large olive-green leaves (split stitch, long and short stitch, straight stitch) CA 1000/10, 7280/2, 7280/4, 7280/6; D 3787; GS 076, 077

3 Red poppy (split stitch, long and short stitch, satin stitch, straight stitch) D 351, 352, 353, 355, 838, 3371, 3770, 3777, 3830, 3857

4 Poppy centre (French knots, straight stitch) CA 5370/2, 5370/4, 5370/6, 5370/10, 9990/6; D 167, 317, 3042, 3743, 3799, 3865

5 Poppy buds (long and short stitch, straight stitch, split stitch) D 351, 352, 353, 355, 3777, 3830; CA 7250/2, 7250/4, 7250/6

6 Vanilla blossoms (long and short stitch, straight stitch, French knots) CA 1000/4; D 317, 352, 353, 3770; GS 076

7 Purple forget-me-nots (French knots) CA 5370/2, 5370/4, 5370/6, 5370/10, 7280/4; GS 076

8 Stems (split stitch) D 3022

9 Small gold leaves (fly stitch) D 167, 3045, 3046, 3047

10 Small olive leaves (fly stitch) CA 1000/10, 7280/4; D 3022, 3046

11 Small grey-green leaves (fly stitch) CA 7250/8, 7940/6; D 318, 3022

12 Strokes (stem stitch, split stitch, satin stitch) D 351, 355, 838; CA 5370/10, 9990/6

METHOD

Copy the design onto the fabric by your preferred method from the tracing outline.

1 Large grey-green leaves

Outline the grey-green leaves in split stitch with one strand CA 7250/4. Fill on either side, starting from the outside in towards the centre vein, with long and short stitch, using one strand each CA 7250/2, 7250/4, 7250/6, 7250/8, 7940/6, D 3787. Shade from light to dark or dark to light, using each shade of green into grey. Stitch the centre vein with split stitch using one strand D 3787. Blend in a few straight stitches of one strand GS 077 at the base of the left leaf to mirror the red in the poppy.

2 Large olive-green leaves

Outline each leaf in split stitch with one strand CA 7280/2. Fill on either side, starting from the outside in towards the centre vein, with long and short stitch, using one strand each CA 1000/10, 7280/2, 7280/4, 7280/6, D 3787. Shade from light to dark or dark to light, using each shade of olive green into dark grey. Stitch the centre vein with split stitch using one strand D 3787. Blend in a few straight stitches using one strand GS 076 and 077 at the base of the left leaf to mirror the red in the poppy.

3 Red poppy

Start with the back petals and work forward. Outline each petal with split stitch using 2 strands D 352. Work from the outside edge in towards the centre. Fill the petals with long and short stitch, using 2 strands in the first row and thereafter one strand, with D 3770, 353, 352, 351, 3830, 355, 3777, 3857. Some of the petals have lighter shades and some darker. Use the photo as a guide. Take one strand 3857 or 838 and blend in a few straight stitches underneath the petals for the shadow. Use one strand 3371 and fill in underneath the petals with satin stitch.

4 Poppy centre

Start at the base with the darkest shade, CA 9990/6, and work a few French knots. Fill the centre with French knots changing to a lighter shade each time. Combine one strand wool and one strand cotton in the needle as follows: CA 5370/2 + D 3743, CA 5370/4 + D 3042, D 317 + CA 5370/6, D 3799 + CA 5370/10. Work a few straight stitches around the centre in D 167 and French knots in one strand D 3865 and 3042. Use the photo as a guide to colour placement.

5 Poppy buds

Fill the flower bud with long and short stitch, shading across and down, using one strand each D 353, 352, 351, 3830, 355, 3777. Outline the lower leaf section in one strand CA 7250/6. Fill with long and short stitch, shading across, using one strand each CA 7250/2, 7250/6, 7250/4. Work a few straight stitches up onto the flower section.

6 Vanilla blossoms

Fill each petal with long and short stitch, shading from light to dark or dark to light, in one strand each CA 1000/4, D 3770, 353, 352, 317. Start with wool and change to cotton. Fill the centre with French knots using 2 strands GS 076.

7 Purple forget-me-nots

Work each flower with clusters of French knots, using one strand of either CA 5370/2, 5370/4, 5370/6 or 5370/10. Work a few French knots in the centre using 2 strands GS 076. Work the flower clusters randomly, filling in gaps between leaves and flowers where necessary. Fill small leaves with straight stitch using one strand CA 7280/4.

8 Stems

Stitch each stem in split stitch using one strand D 3022.

9 Small gold leaves

Use a combination of one strand of each cotton threaded together in the needle: D 3047 + 3045 or D 167 + 3046. Fill each leaf with fly stitch.

10 Small olive leaves on left

Use a combination of one strand each wool and cotton together in the needle, either CA 1000/10 + D 3046 or CA 7280/4 + D 3022. Fill leaves with fly stitch.

11 Small grey-green leaves

Use a combination of one strand each wool and cotton together in the needle, either CA 7250/8 + D 3022 or CA 7940/6 + D 318. Fill all leaves with fly stitch.

12 Stroke work

Fill the red strokes with 2 strands cotton in stem stitch, using the lighter shade D 351 on top and the darker shade D 355 underneath. Stitch the bulb in satin stitch. Take one strand D 838 and stitch a fine line of split stitch underneath as a shadow. Work the dark lavender strokes as for the red, using CA 5370/10 on top and CA 9990/6 underneath.

PROJECT 11: RUSTIC BURGUNDY ROSE

This project is stitched on cream DMC 32 count linen with a medium iron-on interfacing to stabilise the fabric.

Tracing outline

THREAD KEY

Gloriana Lorikeet crewel wool (GW) and DMC stranded cotton (D)

raspberry parfait pastel	GW 091W1
raspberry parfait light	GW 091W2
raspberry parfait	GW 091W3
raspberry parfait dark	GW 091W4
rosewood light	GW 012W2
rosewood dark	GW 012W4
coffee bean dark	GW 166W4
lavender ice pastel	GW 132W1 + D 928
blue heron light	GW 145W2 + D 927
Arctic ice	GW 138W3 + D 926
charcoal light	GW 001W2 +D 3768
green gables light	GW 120W1
forest pastel	GW 87W1
Elizabethan green light	GW 117W2
Elizabethan green	GW 117W3
fresh snow	GW 102W3
lacquered gold pastel	GW 045W1
lacquered gold light	GW 045W2

Gloriana silk (GS)

apricot grove	076
rosewood	012
merry's mauve	122
winter woods	010
fallen leaves	046

DMC metallic (M)

silver	5283

ABBREVIATION KEY

1 Grey leaves (split stitch, long and short stitch) GW 132W1 + D 928, GW 145W2 + D 927, GW 138W3 + D 926, GW 001W2 +D 3768; M 5283

2 Green leaves (split stitch, long and short stitch, straight stitch) GW 87W1, 117W2, 117W3, 120W1; GS 010; M 5283

3 Burgundy rose (split stitch, long and short stitch, satin stitch, straight stitch, French knots) GW 012W2, 012W4, 091W1, 091W2, 091W3, 091W4, 166W4; GS 046

4 Rosebud (split stitch, long and short stitch, straight stitch) GW 87W1, 120W1, 012W2, 012W4, 117W2; GS 010

5 Daisies (split stitch, long and short stitch, straight stitch, French knots) GW 045W1, 045W2, 102W3; GS 010, 076

6 Blossoms (satin stitch, straight stitch, French knots) GW 045W1, 102W3; GS 010, 046, 076

7 Lavender (split stitch, French knots, straight stitch, lazy daisy stitch) GS 012, 076, 122

8 Brown leaves (fly stitch, split stitch) GS 010, 046

9 Small green leaves (long and short stitch) GW 87W1, 117W2

10 Tendrils (stem stitch) GS 012

METHOD

Copy the design onto the fabric by your preferred method from the tracing outline.

1 Grey-green leaves

Outline these four leaves with one line of split stitch in GW 145W2. Fill on either side of the centre vein with long and short stitch, using one strand each wool and cotton together in the needle as follows: GW 132W1 + D 928, GW 145W2 + D 927, GW 138W3 + D 926, GW 001W2 +D 3768. Work the centre vein in one strand D 3768 in split stitch. Work another line close to this in M 5283 (almost on top of it so that the dark cotton peeps out from behind).

2 Green leaves

Outline the leaves with split stitch in one strand GW 117W2. Fill on either side of the centre vein with long and short stitch, shading using one strand each GW 120W1, 87W1, 117W2, 117W3. Work the centre vein in one strand of the darkest shade of wool in split stitch. Work another line close to this in M 5283. Blend in a few straight stitches using one strand GS 010 as shown in the photo. This reflects the burgundy of the rose in the leaves.

Stitch direction diagram

3 Burgundy rose

Start with the back petals and work forwards. Outline each petal individually in split stitch using one strand GW 091W3. Fill each petal with long and short stitch, using one strand GW 091W1, 091W2, 091W3, 091W4, 012W2, 012W4, 166W4, shading from the outside in towards the centre, from light to dark. The back petals are slightly darker than the front petals and the turnovers are worked in satin stitch in the lightest shade, GW 091W1. The centre sections are worked in satin stitch in GW 166W4. Work a few French knots using 2 strands GS 046. When the petals are complete go back and add in a few straight stitches GW 166W4 under the turnovers and at the bases to emphasise the shadows

4 Rosebud

Outline the bud with split stitch using one strand GW 012W4 and fill with long and short stitch using one strand 012W4 and 012W2. Outline the sepals with split stitch using one strand 117W2. Fill the base with one strand 87W1 and work a few straight stitches in 117W2. Fill the sepals with long and short stitch using one strand 117W2 and work a few straight stitches at the base in one strand GS 010. Work split stitch alongside each sepal and the tips in GS 010.

5 Daisies

Outline all the petals in split stitch using one strand GW 045W2. Start with the back petals and fill each petal with long and short stitch, shading from light to dark using one strand each 102W3, 045W1, 045W2. Work a few straight stitches in one strand GS 076 at the base. Fill the centre with French knots using 2 strands GS 010.

6 Blossoms

Work the gold blossoms in satin stitch using one strand GW 045W1, work a few straight stitches in the centre using one strand GS 010. Fill the centre with French knots using 2 strands GS 076. Work the white blossoms as before in GW 102W3 with a few straight stitches in GS 046, and fill the centres in French knots in GS 076.

7 Lavender sprays

Work the stems in split stitch using one strand GS 076. Work the leaves in lazy daisy stitches using 2 strands 076 with one straight stitch in the centre. Work the flowers in French knots using one strand each of 012 + 122 together in the needle.

8 Brown leaves

Work the veins and stems in split stitch using one strand GS 010. Work each leaf in fly stitch using 2 strands of either 010 or 046. The darker leaves will be at the bottom.

9 Small green leaves

Fill each leaf with long and short stitch using one strand each GW 87W1 and 117W2.

10 Tendrils

Work the tendrils with stem stitch in one strand GS 012.

PROJECT 12: MAUVE AND WHITE ROSE SPRAY

This project has been stitched on a natural linen twill fabric.

Tracing outline

Appleton crewel wool (AP)

white	991
pale chocolate	181
light mauve	601
med mauve	603
dark dull mauve	933
putty brown	983
pale yellow	872
light honeysuckle	692
med honeysuckle	693
very pale green	873
pale grey green	351
light mid olive	343
med drab green	334
med Jacobean green	292
dark Jacobean green	291
dark elephant grey	975

Gumnut Blossoms crewel wool (GW)

very pale pansy	231

Gumnut Buds perle (GP)

eucalypt	626

Caron Watercolours cotton (CW)

vanilla	098
kelp	139
Gobi sand	082

Caron Waterlilies silk (CS)

antique rose	108

DMC stranded cotton (D)

pale mauve grey	453
light mauve grey	452
dark mauve grey	3860
very dark mauve	779
pale mauve	3743
light mauve	3042
dark mauve	3740
pale plum	3836
light plum	3835
cream	746
light gold	3047
med gold	3046
dark gold	3045
very dark gold	829

DMC rayon (R)

white	35200

DMC metallic (M)

gold	5282

1 Large olive-green leaves (split stitch, long and short stitch) AP 343, 334, 351, 873; M 5282

2 Large Jacobean green leaves (split stitch, long and short stitch) AP 291, 292, 975; M 5282; D 829.

3 Small leaves (fly stitch) AP 343.

4 Large white rose petals (split stitch, long and short stitch, straight stitch) AP 181, 601, 991; R 35200; D 452, 453, 779; GW 231

5 Large white rose centre (French knots) AP 692, 872, 991; D 746, 779, 3045, 3047, 3860

6 Large mauve rose (split stitch, long and short stitch, satin stitch, straight stitch) AP 181, 231, 601, 603; D 779, 3042, 3740, 3743, 3835, 3836

7 Three medium cream flowers (long and short stitch, straight stitch, French knots) AP 692, 693, 872, 983, 991, 933; D 746, 779, 3045, 3046, 3047, 3860, 5282; M 5282

8 Small white flowers (granitos, straight stitch, French knots, lazy daisy stitch) CW 098; AP 693, 933, 983; M 5282; D 3042

9 Stems (split stitch) GP 626

10 Small leaves (fly stitch, lazy daisy stitch) CW 139

11 Lavender sprays (lazy daisy stitch) AP 603; CS 108

12 Grasses (straight stitch) CW 082

Stitch direction diagram

Copy the design onto the fabric by your preferred method from the tracing outline.

1 Large olive-green leaves

Outline each leaf with split stitch using one strand AP 343. Fill each side of the leaves with long and short stitch, using one strand each AP 873, 351, 343, 334, from the outside edge in towards the centre. Shade from light to dark or dark to light on either side. Work the centre vein in split stitch using one strand M 5282.

2 Large Jacobean green leaves

Outline each leaf with split stitch using one strand AP 291. Fill each side of the leaves with long and short from the outside edge in towards the centre, using one strand each AP 292, 291, 975. Work a few straight stitches using one strand AP 829 on one side of each leaf. Work the centre vein in split stitch using one strand M 5282.

3 Small leaves

Work the leaves in fly stitch using one strand AP 343.

4 Large white rose petals

Outline each petal in split stitch using one strand AP 991. Work the back petals first and remember to use dark shading underneath the overlaps. Using a combination of one strand wool and one strand rayon or cotton, fill each petal with long and short stitch using 2 strands together in the needle as follows: AP 991 + R 35200, AP 181 + D 453, AP 601 + D 452, GW 231 + R 35200, shading from light to dark in the centre. Take one strand D 779 and work split and straight stitches underneath the overlaps of the petals to create shadows.

5 Large white rose centre

Work straight stitches at the base of the petals and slightly up underneath the overlaps using one strand each D 3860 and D 779. Fill the centre with French knots, using one strand wool and cotton together in the needle as follows: AP 991 + D 746, AP 872 + D 3047, AP 692 + D 3045.

6 Large mauve rose

Outline each section of the rose in split stitch using one strand AP 601. Start with the back petals and fill with long and short stitch, using one strand wool and cotton together in the needle as follows: AP

231+ D 3743, AP 181 + D 3042, AP 601 + D 3836, AP 603 + D 3835. Remember to use darker shades under the overlaps. Work the dark centres and turnover in satin stitch using one strand D 3740 or AP 231. Using one strand D 779 work a few straight stitches to accent the shadowed areas.

7 Three medium cream flowers

Fill each petal with long and short stitch, using one strand of wool and cotton together in the needle as follows: AP 991 + D 746, AP 872 + D 3047, AP 692 + D 3046. Work a few straight stitches in the centre using one strand each D 3045, 3860 and AP 693.

Fill the centre with French knots using a combination of one strand each wool and metallic gold as follows: AP 933 + M 5282, AP 983 + D 5282.

8 Small white flowers

Work the larger flowers in granitos using one strand CW 098. Using one strand of CW 3042, work a few straight stitches in the centre of each petal. Fill the centre with French knots using a combination of one strand each wool and cotton: M 5282 + AP 693.

Work the smaller flowers in lazy daisy stitch using one strand CW 098. Fill the centre with French knots using a combination of one strand each AP 933 + AP 983.

9 Stems

Work each grass bud with 2 straight stitches, applied randomly along the stalks in one strand GP 626.

10 Small leaves

Work all the small leaves in fly stitch using one strand CW 139. Work a lazy daisy stitch for the very small leaves in CW 139.

11 Lavender buds

Work each bud in lazy daisy stitch using a combination of one strand each AP 603 + CS 108. Work a straight stitch in the centre of each in 2 strands CS 108.

12 Grasses

Work all stems in split stitch using one strand CW 082.

ADVANCED LEVEL

The following five projects are more suited to the embroiderer who has some experience of long and short stitch embroidery and is able to follow the placement of colours as listed.

Project 13: Golden flowers

This project is stitched on off-white Belgian linen.

Tracing outline

THREAD KEY

DMC stranded cotton (D)

cream	3823
pale green gold	834
med green gold	832
dark green gold	830
grey brown	3781
dark brown	3021
light gold	676
med gold	729
dark gold	782
very dark gold	780
dark gold brown	869
light grey green	3023
med grey green	522
light gold brown	612
med gold brown	610
off white	712

Gloriana Lorikeet crewel wool (GW)
plus DMC stranded cotton (D)

soft white	GW 000W1 + D blanc
pecan pastel	GW 133W1 + D 712
pecan light	GW 133W2 + D 677
pecan	GW 133W3 + D 676
vanilla	GW 003W3 +D 712
lacquered gold pastel	GW 045W1 + D 677
lacquered gold light	GW 045W2 + D 676

Caron Watercolours cotton (CW)

honeysuckle	132

Gloriana silk (GS)

winter woods	010
lacquered gold	045
woodpond	049

DMC metallic (M)

gold	5282

Stitch direction diagram

ABBREVIATION KEY

1 Large brassy gold leaves (split stitch, long and short stitch, straight stitch) D 676, 729, 780, 782, 869, 3021, 3823; M 5282

2 Large green-gold leaves (split stitch, long and short stitch, straight stitch) D 830, 832, 834, 3021, 3781, 3823; M 5282

3 Large dark gold flower (split stitch, long and short stitch, straight stitch) D 612, 712, 830; GW 133W1 + D 712, GW 133W2 + D 677, GW 133W3 + D 676, GW 000W1 + D blanc

4 Flower centre (straight stitch, satin stitch, French knots) D 676, 712, 729, 780, 782, 3021; GS 010, 049

5 Large light gold flower (split stitch, long and short stitch, straight stitch) GW 000W1 + D blanc, GW 003W3 + D 712, GW 045W1 + D 677, GW 045W2 + D 676; D 522, 712, 729, 3023

6 Flower centre (straight stitch, satin stitch, French knots) D 676, 712, 729, 780, 782, 3021; GS 010, 049

7 White blossoms (straight stitch, French knots) CW 132; D 676, 782, 3823

8 Small green leaves (fly stitch) GS 049

9 Medium gold leaves (fly stitch) GS 045

10 Stems (split stitch) D 830, 3021

11 Lavender (bullions) GS 010

12 Buds (long and short stitch, straight stitch) D 610, 612, 712, 3023

METHOD

Copy the design onto the fabric by your preferred method from the tracing outline.

1 Large brassy gold leaves

Start with the leaves at the back and work forward. Outline each leaf in split stitch using 2 strands D 729. Fill on either side of the centre vein with long and short stitch, starting from the outside edge in towards the centre vein. Start with 2 strands of cotton, using a combination of D 3823 + 676 for the light shade, then change to one strand, shading with 729, 782, 780, 869, 3021. You will need to use one or two shades in each row. On the other side of the leaf start with the darker shades and blend through to the light shades. Using one strand 3021, work a line of split stitch down the centre vein and work a few straight stitches towards this line to accent the shadowed areas. Work a line of split stitch in M 5282 close to the dark brown line.

2 Large green-gold leaves

Start with the leaves at the back and work forward. Outline each leaf in D 834 using 2 strands. Fill on either side of the centre vein with long and short stitch, working from the outside in towards the centre vein. Start with 2 strands of cotton, using a combination of 3823 + 834 for the light shade, then change to one strand and shade with 832, 830, 3781, 3021. You will need to use one or two shades in each row. On the other side of the leaf start with the darker shades and blend through to the light shades. Using one strand of 3021 work a line of split stitch down the centre vein and work a few straight stitches towards this line to accent the shadowed areas. Work a line of split stitch in M 5282 close to the dark brown line.

3 Large dark gold flower (at base)

Start with the back petals and work forward. Outline each petal with split stitch using one strand GW 133W1. Fill the petals with long and short stitch, starting from the outside edge in towards the centre (or underneath the turnover towards the centre). Shade from dark to light or light to dark, using the photo as a guide. You will need to use one strand of wool and one strand of cotton together in the needle as follows: GW 133W1 + D 712, GW 133W2 + D 677, GW 133W3 + D 676, GW 000W1 + D blanc. Take one strand each D 830 and D 612 and work a few straight stitches in the shadowed areas to add emphasis, especially under the turnovers. Outline the turnovers with split stitch using one strand GW 000W1, and pad inside with one strand of wool. Using one strand D 712, fill the turnovers with slanted satin stitch.

4. Flower centre

Use the photo as a guide to colour placement. Pad around the circle with straight stitch using 2 strands cotton or one strand leftover wool. Outline the circle in split stitch using one strand D 780. Cover the circle with straight satin stitch, working from the outside in towards the inner circle edge using one strand D 780, 782, 729 adjacent to each other. Outline the inner circle edge in split stitch with one strand D 3021 and make a few straight stitches over the circle out towards the edge of the centre at intervals. Fill the inner circle with French knots, using one strand each 676 + 729 together in the needle, slightly covering the dark line. Scatter loose French knots around the edge of the circle and slightly over the petals using one strand D 712 + 676, GS 010 or 049 at intervals.

5 Large light gold flower

Start with the back petals and work forward. Outline each petal with split stitch using one strand GW 000W1. Fill the petals with long and short stitch, starting from the outside edge in towards the centre (or underneath the turnover towards the centre). Shade from dark to light, or light to dark, using the photo as a guide, with one strand wool and one strand cotton together in the needle as follows: GW 000W1 + D blanc, GW 003W3 + D 712, GW 045W1 + D 677, GW 045W2 + D 676. Take one strand each D 3023 and D 522 and work a few straight stitches in the shadowed areas to add emphasis, especially under the turnovers. Outline the turnovers with split stitch using one strand GW 000W1 and pad inside with one strand of wool. Using one strand D 712, fill the turnovers with slanted satin stitch.

6 Flower centre

Work as for the other centre (see 4).

7 White blossoms

Fill each petal with one strand of CW 132, working straight stitches from the centre out towards the outside edge. Work a few on top to give a plump look. Using one strand D 3823, work a few straight stitches at the base of each petal. Using a combination of one strand each D 676 + 782 in the needle, work French knots in the centre. Make a few straight stitches between the petals using 782.

8 Small green leaves

Fill the small leaves with fly stitch, using 2 strands GS 049.

9 Medium gold leaves

Fill the medium leaves with fly stitch, using 2 strands GS 045.

10 Stems

Work all the stems in split stitch using one strand D 830. On the thicker stems add a second line of split stitch in D 3021 as a shadow.

11 Lavender

Work bullions using about 7 wraps in 2 strands GS 010.

12 Buds

Outline each bud with split stitch using one strand D 712. Pad each bud with one strand of some leftover cream wool, making straight stitches across the bud. Fill the buds with long and short stitch, using one strand each D 712, 3023. Work a few straight stitches in D 610 and 612 to create shadows along the sides and base, and then work a few straight stitches at the top of each bud.

PROJECT 14: WHITE POPPY WITH BLUE BERRIES

This project has been stitched on DMC natural 32 count linen with a medium iron-on interfacing to stabilise the fabric.

Tracing outline

Stitch direction diagram

Gloriana Lorikeet crewel wool (GW)

lacquered gold pastel	045W1
lacquered gold light	045W2
pecan	133W3
pecan dark	133W4
Spanish moss pastel	048W1
Spanish moss light	048W2
Spanish moss	048W3
forest light	87W2
Elizabethan green light	117W2
fresh snow	102W3
vanilla	003W3
lavender ice pastel	132W1
Arctic ice pastel	138W1
blue heron light	145W2
Arctic ice light	138W2
Arctic ice	138W3

Gloriana silk (GS) (alternative)

charcoal	001	(DMC 3799)
slate green	051	(DMC 640)

DMC stranded cotton (D)

white	blanc
pale teal blue	927
light teal blue	926
med teal blue	3768
dark blue	930
very dark black brown	3371
dark grey brown	3787
very dark grey brown	3021
light gold	677
med gold	3045
med coffee brown	3790
dark coffee brown	3781

1   Large green leaves (split stitch, long and short stitch, satin stitch, straight stitch) GW 048W1, 048W2, 048W3, 87W2, 117W2; D 3021, 3787

2   Large gold leaves (split stitch, long and short stitch, satin stitch, straight stitch) GW 045W1, 045W2, 048W2, 133W3, 133W4; D 3021, 3781

3   Blue berries (split stitch, long and short stitch, straight stitch) D blanc, 926, 927, 930, 3371, 3768; GS 001

4   Large white blue flower (split stitch, long and short stitch, satin stitch, straight stitch) GW 003W3, 102W3, 132W1, 138W1, 138W2, 138W3, 145W2; D 3787; GS 051

5   Flower centre (French knots) D 677, 926, 3045, 3371, 3787, 3790; GW 045W1, 045W2, 133W3

6   Small white blue flower (split stitch, long and short stitch) GW 048W2, 87W2, 102W3, 117W2, 132W1, 138W1, 138W2, 145W2; GS 051

7   Stems and small leaves (split stitch, long and short stitch, satin stitch) D 3021, 3787; GW 87W2, 048W1, 048W2, 048W3

METHOD

Copy the design onto the fabric by your preferred method from the tracing outline.

1 Large green leaves

Start with the back leaves and work forward. Outline each leaf in split stitch using one strand GW 048W3. Start from the outside edge in towards the centre vein and shade from light to dark or dark to light. Fill each leaf with long and short stitch, using one strand each GW 048W1, 048W2, 048W3, 87W2, 117W2 (you can use 2 strands in the first row). Work a few straight stitches in one strand D 3787 to accentuate the shadowed areas. Using one strand D 3021, work the centre vein in split stitch. Work another line close to this using one strand GW 048W2. Stitch the turnover in padded satin stitch using one strand GW 048W1.

2 Large golden green leaves

Start with the back leaves and work forward. Outline each leaf in split stitch using one strand GW 133W3. Start from the outside edge in towards the centre vein and shade from light to dark or dark to light. Fill each leaf with long and short stitch using one strand each GW 045W1, 045W2, 133W3, 133W4, 048W2 (you can use 2 strands on the first row—the green can be worked together with the gold in the first row). Work a few straight stitches in one strand D 3781 to accentuate the shadowed areas. Using one strand D 3021 work the centre vein in split stitch. Stitch a second line close to this in one strand GW 045W2.

3 Blue berries

Use the step-by-step photos as a guide. Start with the berries at the back and work forward. Outline each berry as you go along with split stitch in 2 strands D 926. Start at the base of the berry with GS 001 and D 3371, using one strand, and shade from dark to light towards the tip, using D 930, 3768, 926, 927, blanc. Finally, make a few small straight stitches at the centre of each berry using one strand 3371.

4 Large white/blue flower

Use the photo as a guide; some petals are darker than others. Start with the back petals and work forward. Outline each petal with split stitch as you go along, using one strand GW 102W3. Starting from the outside edge in towards the centre, fill each petal with long and short stitch, shading with one strand each GW 102W3, 003W3, 132W1, 138W1, 145W2, 138W2, 138W3 (you can use 2 strands in the first row, and stitch alternate colours in some rows to fit in all the shades). Using one strand GS 051, work a few straight stitches to accentuate shadows, then take one strand D 3787 and work in a few more straight stitches to deepen the shadows. Work any turnovers in padded satin stitch using one strand GW 003W3.

5 Flower centre

Use a combination of one strand wool and one strand cotton together in the needle as follows: GW 045W1 + D 677, GW 045W2 + D 3045, GW 133W3 + D 3790. Fill the centre with French knots, shading from dark at the base to light at the top. Scatter loose French knots around the centre starting with D 3371, then 3787, 926.

6 Small white/blue flower

Outline each petal with split stitch using one strand GW 102W3. Start with the back petals and work forward. Fill each petal with long and short stitch, shading from the outside in towards the centre using one strand each GW 102W3, 132W1, 138W1, 145W2, 138W2. Use the photo as a guide; some of the back petals are in dark shades, and the front are lighter. Add a few straight stitches at the base of the petals in GS 051. Outline each leaf of the calyx with split stitch using one strand GW 87W2, then fill with long and short stitch using one strand each GW 048W2, 87W2, 117W2, shading down towards the base.

7 Stems and small leaves

Work each stem in split stitch, using one strand D 3787, and working another line close to this in one strand 3021. Fill the larger leaves with long and short stitch, using one strand each GW 048W1, 048W2, 048W3, 87W2, towards the centre vein. Fill the small leaves with satin stitch, using one strand of either GW 048W1 or 048W2 on the light side and 048W3 or 87W2 on the darker side.

PROJECT 15: DOG ROSES WITH RIBBON AND DAISIES

This project has been stitched on off-white Belgian linen.

Permission granted by Gretchen Cagle Publications, Inc. for adaptation of Gretchen Cagle's design, 'The heart basket', previously published in *Heart to Heart: Rose Petals, Heart Strings, and Other Things* (copyright 1988).

Tracing outline

THREAD KEY
DMC stranded cotton (D)

pale peach	353
light peach	352
med peach	351
dark peach	3830
very dark peach	355
dark rust	3858
very dark rust	3857
dark brown	938
very dark brown	3371
cream	746
pale flesh	951
light flesh	3856
light rust	402
light terracotta	3778
med terracotta	356
med plum	3722
dark plum	3721
dark plum brown	632
dark coffee brown	898
pale orange	3855
light orange	3854
med orange rust	3776
dark orange rust	975

Gloriana Lorikeet crewel wool (GW)

taupe	105W3
Spanish moss pastel	048W1
Spanish moss light	048W2
Spanish moss	048W3
forest light	87W2
taupe dark	105W4
forest pastel	87W1
fresh snow	102W3
sterling silver pastel	005W1
denim blue pastel	155W1
denim blue light	155W2

Gloriana silk (GS)

slate green	051
highland meadow	040

Stitch direction diagram

ABBREVIATION KEY

1 Ribbon (long and short stitch) D 351, 352, 353, 355, 938, 3371, 3830, 3857, 3858

2 Golden green leaves (long and short stitch, split, straight stitch) GW 87W2, 048W1, 048W2, 048W3, 105W3; D 898, 975

3 Grey-green leaves (long and short stitch, split stitch, straight stitch) GW 87W1, 105W3, 105W4; GS 051; D 356, 402, 746, 898, 951, 975, 3778, 3856

4 Daisies (long and short stitch) GW 005W1, 102W3, 155W1, 155W2

5 Daisy centre (French knots) D 898, 975, 3371, 3776, 3854, 3855

6 Large dog roses (long and short stitch, split stitch, straight stitch, satin stitch) D 356, 402, 632, 746, 898, 938, 951, 3371, 3721, 3722, 3778, 3856, 3857, 3858

7 Rose centre (French knots) D 898, 975, 3371, 3776, 3854, 3855

8 Rosebuds (long and short stitch, straight stitch, split stitch) D 975, 3721 3857, 3858; GW 87W1

9 Grasses (French knots, split stitch) GS 040; D 975

10 Small leaves and stems (fly stitch, split stitch) GS 051; GW 87W1; D 975

METHOD

Copy the design onto the fabric by your preferred method from the tracing outline.

1 Ribbon

Do not outline the ribbon with split stitch. Start at the top of each ribbon section and work down in long and short stitch, shading from dark to light and back to dark under the turnovers. Use 2 strands in the first row and one strand thereafter as follows: D 353, 352, 351, 3830, 355, 3858, 3857, 938, 3371.

2 Golden green leaves

Outline the leaves with split stitch in one strand GW 048W1. Start from the outside edge and work towards the centre vein in long and short stitch, keeping in line with the guidelines. Shade from dark to light or light to dark using 2 strands in the first row and one strand thereafter as follows: GW 105W3, 048W1, 048W2, 048W3, 87W2. Work the centre vein in split stitch using one strand D 898 and another row close to this in D 975.

3 Grey-green leaves

Outline the leaves with split stitch in one strand GW 105W4. Start from the outside edge and work towards the centre vein in long and short stitch, keeping in line with the guidelines. Shade from dark to light, or light to dark, using 2 strands in the first row and one strand thereafter as follows: GW 105W3, 105W4, 87W1. Add a few highlights on each leaf by blending in one strand each D 746, 951, 3856, 402, 3778, 356 (this is optional). Work the centre vein in split stitch using one strand D 898 and another row close to this in D 975.

4 Daisies

Do not outline the petals. Fill each petal with long and short stitch using one strand each GW 102W3, 005W1, 155W1, 155W2, shading from soft white through to dark blue.

5 Daisy centre

Fill the centre with French knots using 2 strands each D 3855, 3854, 3776, 975, 898. Start with the darkest shade of brown and work up to the lightest. Take one strand D 3371 and work a few loose knots around the centre.

6 Large dog roses

Start with the petal that is furthest back. Outline each petal with split stitch using 2 strands D 3856. Fill each petal with long and short stitch, using 2 strands in the first row and one strand thereafter. Start from the outside edge in towards the centre (or from under the turnover) using D 746, 951, 3856, 402, 3778, 356, 3722, 3721, 632, 898, 3858, 3857, 938 (you can alternate 2 colours in a row sometimes to fit in the shades). Use the photo as a guide as some petals are darker and some lighter. For the turnovers work a line of split stitch under the turnover using one strand 3857, then make a few straight stitches into the split stitch edge in 3857 and 938 to add a shadow underneath the turnover. Work the turnover in padded satin stitch using one strand 746.

7 Rose centres

Fill the centres with French knots using 2 strands each D 3855, 3854, 3776, 975, 898. Start with the darkest shade of brown and work up to the lightest. Take one strand of 3371 and work a few loose knots around the centre.

8 Rosebuds

Work the bud in long and short stitch, using one strand each D 3721, 3857, 3858. Outline the sepals in split stitch using one strand GW 87W1, and fill with long and short stitch in 87W1. Take one strand D 975 and blend in a few straight stitches to add shadows, and work a few straight lines next to the sepal tips.

9 Grasses

Stitch the stems in split stitch using one strand D 975. Using 2 strands GS 040, scatter French knots around the stems.

10 Small leaves and stems

Work all the stems in split stitch using one strand D 975. Work the small leaves in fly stitch, using one strand each GS 051 + GW 87W1 together in the needle.

PROJECT 16: DOG ROSES WITH GRASSES AND FLOWERS

This project is stitched on off-white linen union with an iron-on interfacing to stabilise the fabric.

Tracing outline

Stitch direction diagram

THREAD KEY

Appleton crewel wool (AP)

med bright terracotta	225
dark bright terracotta	226
dark dull rose pink	147
very dark dull rose pink	149
dark wine red	716
pale rose pink	751
light rose pink	753
med rose pink	754
dark rose pink	755
putty grounding brown	986
pale yellow pastel	871
light honeysuckle yellow	693
white	991
pale wine red	711
light wine red	712
med dull rose pink	145
pale grey green	351
light Jacobean green	292
med Jacobean green	294
dark elephant grey	975
light drab green	331
light mid olive green	342
medium mid olive green	344
dark olive green	243
very dark olive green	245

Gumnut Blossoms crewel wool (GB)

pale pink	173
light pink	231
medium pink	232

Gloriana Lorikeet crewel wool (GW)

forest light	87W2
Spanish moss light	048W2
pigeon pastel	140W1

Gloriana silk (GS)

winter woods	010
harvest grape	112

Gumnut Buds perle (GP)

pale khaki	641
light khaki	643

Caron Watercolours cotton (CW)

camouflage	047
cinnabar	164

DMC stranded cotton (D)

(blending colours marked with * can
    be omitted if necessary)

dark coral pink	3328*
dark pink	3831*
very dark pink	777*
very dark maroon	154
very dark brown	3371
pale pink	225*
med coral pink	760*
maroon	3685*
med plum pink	316*
dark plum pink	3803*
dark grape	3834
dark gold	167
pale gold	3047
med gold	422
very dark gold	869
off white	3865*
light plum	3727*
pale grey green	524*
med grey green	522*
med brown grey	640*
dark brown grey	3787
light khaki	613*
med khaki	612*
med khaki green	3012*
dark khaki green	3011*
very dark grey	844
pale dull mauve	3743
light dull mauve	3042
med dull mauve	3041
dark dull mauve	779

ABBREVIATION KEY

1. Large grey-green leaves (split stitch, long and short stitch, straight stitch) AP 292, 294, 351, 975; D 522, 524, 640, 844, 3371, 3787; GS 010

2. Large olive leaves (split stitch, long and short stitch, straight stitch) AP 243, 245, 331, 342, 344; D 612, 613, 844, 3011, D 3012, D 3787

3. Red rose at top right (split stitch, long and short stitch) AP 225, 226, 147, 149, 716; D 154, 777, 3328, 3371, 3831; GW 048W2, 87W2

4. Large pink/red rose at left (split stitch, long and short stitch) AP 147, 751, 753, 754, 755; D 225, 316, 760, 844, 3685, 3803, 3834

5. Large rose centres (French knots, straight stitch) D 167, 422, 844, 869, 3042, 3047; AP 693, 871, 986

6. Large white/mauve rose (split stitch, long and short stitch, straight stitch, satin stitch) AP 145, 711, 712, 991; D 316, 779, 844, 3727, 3743, 3803, 3834, 3865; GB 173, 231, 232

7. Small mauve flowers (long and short stitch, French knots, fly stitch, split stitch, straight stitch) AP 693, 871; D 779, 869, 3041, 3042, 3047; GW 140W1; GS 112

8. Small daisies (lazy daisy stitch, straight stitch, French knots) CW 047, 164; GP 643

9. Wheat stalks (satin stitch, split, long and short stitch) GP 641, 643; D 422, 844, 869

10. Grasses (split stitch, French knots) GS 010, 112

11. Main stems (split stitch) GW 048W2, 87W2

METHOD

Copy the design onto the fabric by your preferred method from the tracing outline.

1 Large grey-green leaves

Outline the leaves with split stitch in one strand AP 292. Fill each side of the leaf with long and short from the outside edge in towards the centre vein, shading from light to dark or dark to light with one strand each of wool and cotton together in the needle as follows: AP 351 + D 524, AP 292 + D 522, AP 294 + D 640, AP 975 + D 3787. Blend in single strands of D 844 and 3371 to indicate the shadowed area. Add a few straight stitches, blended in on top in GS 010, to give a rusty highlight. Work the centre vein in split stitch using one strand D 3371 and then a second line close to this in D 524.

2 Large olive leaves

Outline the leaves with split stitch in one strand AP 342. Fill each side of the leaf with long and short from the outside edge in towards the centre vein, shading from light to dark or dark to light with one strand each of wool and cotton together in the needle as follows: AP 331 + D 613, AP 342 + D 612, AP 344 + D 3012, AP 243 + D 3011, AP 245 + D 844. Blend in one strand D 3787 to indicate the shadowed area. Work the centre vein in split stitch

using one strand 3787 and a second close to this in D 613.

3 Red rose at top right

Outline all petals with split stitch in one strand AP 147. Starting with the back petals, fill with long and short stitch, shading from light to dark towards the centre base. Use one strand of wool and cotton together in the needle as follows: AP 225 + D 3328, AP 226 + D 3831, AP 147 + D 777, AP 149 + D 154. Blend in a few straight stitches in one strand AP 716 and then D 3371 at the base. Use the photo as a guide some of the petals are worked in dark shades and some lighter shades. Work all the shadowed areas underneath the petals with one strand of split stitch in D 3371 to give emphasis. Fill the base leaves with long and short stitch using one strand of GW 87W2 and 048W2.

4 Large pink/red rose at left

Outline each petal with split stitch using one strand AP 753. Fill each petal with long and short stitch shading from light to dark (or dark to light) towards the centre base. Use one strand wool and cotton together in the needle as follows: AP 751 + D 225, AP 753 + D 760, AP 754 + D316. Change to one strand of AP 755, D 316, 3803, 3834 at the base. Use the photo as a guide some of the petals are worked in darker shades and some in lighter. Work all the shadowed areas underneath the petals with split stitch in one strand D 844 to give emphasis.

5 Large rose centres

Work around the outside of the centre circle with straight stitches in a combination of one strand each together in the needle of D 844 + D 3042. These straight stitches must encroach into the petals slightly. Start working French knots inside the circle, shading from dark to light in the centre with a combination of one strand wool and cotton together in the needle of AP 986 + D 167, AP 693 + D 422, AP 871 + D 3047. Work the stamens in random straight stitches in one strand D 869. Work random loose French knots at the end of the stamens and scattered in between with one strand D 167, 422.

6 Large white/mauve rose at front

Outline each petal with split stitch in one strand AP 991. Fill each petal with long and short stitch shading from light to dark (or dark to light) towards the centre base. Use one strand each together in the needle as follows: AP 991 + D 3865, GB 231 + D 3865, GB 232 + D 3743, AP 711 + D 3727, AP 712 + D 316, AP 145 + D 3803. Use the photo as a guide, as some petals are darker and some lighter. Blend in one strand of D 3834 at the base of each petal to give it depth. Work the petal turnovers in satin stitch in GB 173. Work all the shadowed areas underneath the petals with one strand D 844 in split stitch. Work a line of split stitch under the turnovers in one strand 844 and blend in a few straight stitches towards this line in D 779 to create a shadow.

7 Small mauve flowers

Work all the petals in long and short stitch, shading from light to dark (or dark to light) in the centre, using one strand each GW 140W1, D 3042, 3041. Emphasise the shadowed areas with one strand D 779 in straight or split stitch. Fill the flower centre with French knots in a combination of one strand each of AP 871 + D 3047, AP 693 + D 869, shading from dark to light at the top. Work the leaves in fly stitch using 2 strands GS 112.

8 Very small daisy flowers

Work the petals in lazy daisy stitch using one strand CW 164 or CW 047, adding a straight stitch in the centre of each. Work one flower of each pair in 164 and one in 047. Fill the centre with French knots in one strand GP 164.

9 Wheat stalks

Outline each grain with split stitch and lay a loose foundation of satin stitch in each to raise the top sti--t the base of each grain in D 422 and 869. Work split stitch shadows under each grain using one strand D 844. Work the stem in split stitch using one strand D 869. Add the whiskers by stitching long straight stitches in one strand D 422.

10 Grasses

Work the stems in split stitch in one strand GS 010 and scatter French knots randomly about the branches in GS 112, using 2 strands.

11 Main stems

Work the stems in split stitch using 2 strands GW 87W2, 048W2. Vary the colours in each stem,

PROJECT 17: YELLOW POPPIES ON NAVY BLUE BACKGROUND

This project was stitched on navy blue Belgian linen. I dyed off-white linen to get the colour I wanted; you could use black if you prefer.

The dark background in this project tends to show through the stitching slightly, especially where light coloured threads are used. To overcome this problem, which is common to dark backgrounds, I used a white opaque fabric paint, which I have watered down, to fill in large areas such as the poppy petals and the large leaves. Be careful not to make the paint too thick as it will leave a hard surface which is difficult to stitch through. The paint coverage will result in a lighter shade of blue; it will not be completely white. Follow the directions on the fabric paint bottle and iron the fabric on the back when the paint is dry.

THREAD KEY

Appleton crewel wool (AP)

bright white	991B
custard yellow	851
pale grey green	351
light grey green	352
light Jacobean green	292
med Jacobean green	293
pale mid olive green	341
light mid olive green	342
med mid olive green	345
dark elephant grey	975

Gloriana Lorikeet crewel wool (GW)

vanilla	003W3
vanilla dark	003W4

DMC stranded cotton (D)

white	blanc
vanilla	739
dark vanilla	738
light custard yellow	3855
light burnt orange	3827
med burnt orange	977
med brown	3790
dark grey brown	3787
very dark brown	3371

light teal green	928
med teal green	927
dark teal green	926
very dark teal green	3768
very dark grey	3799
light grey green	524
med grey green	522
med brown grey	642
dark brown grey	640
pale taupe	3866
pale mauve	153
light mauve	3836
med mauve	3835
dark mauve	3834
light mauve pink	3727

Gloriana silk (GS)

winter woods	010
seaweed	088

Caron Watercolours cotton (CW)

tiffany rose	030
vanilla	098
monsoon	197

DMC metallic (M)

blue grey	E317

Tracing outline

ABBREVIATION KEY

1 Large drab green leaves (split stitch, long and short stitch, straight stitch) AP 341, 342, 345, 975; D 3727, 3787; GS 010; M E317

2 Large grey-green leaves (split stitch, long and short stitch, straight stitch) AP 292, 293, 351, 352; D 3787, 3855; GS 088; M E317

3 Large poppies (split stitch, long and short stitch, straight stitch) AP 851, 991B; GW 003W3, 003W4, D blanc, 738, 739, 977, 3790, 3787, 3827, 3855

4 Poppy centres (split stitch, long and short stitch, straight stitch, French knots) D 522, 524, 926, 927, 928, 3371, 3768, 3787, 3799, 3827, 3855

5 Pink blossoms (split stitch, long and short stitch, French knots) D 153, 3834, 3835, 3790, 3836, 3866; AP 851

6 Small white blossoms (straight stitch, French knots) CW 030, 098; D 3371, 3790, 3835, 3836

7 Large teal leaves (fly stitch) CW 197

8 Small olive leaves (fly stitch) AP 341, 975; D 640, 642

9 Stems (split stitch, stem stitch) D 640, 642

10 Buds (padded satin stitch, split stitch) GW 030

11 Grasses (French knots) GW 030

METHOD

Copy the design onto the fabric by your preferred method from the tracing outline.

1 Large drab green leaves

Outline the leaves with split stitch using one strand AP 342. Fill on either side of the centre vein with long and short stitch, shading from light to dark (or dark to light) using one strand each AP 341, 342, 345, 975 and D 3787. Work the centre vein in split stitch using one strand D 3787 then work another line close to this in M E317. Blend in straight stitches on top of the leaf stitching, using one strand GS 010, and then add some D 3727 to reflect the pink in the small flowers. Use the photo as a guide to placement of colour.

2 Large grey-green leaves

Outlines the leaves with split stitch using one strand AP 352. Fill on either side of the centre vein with long and short stitch, shading from light to dark (or dark to light) in one strand each AP 351, 352, 292, 293. Work the centre vein in split stitch using one strand D 3787 then work another line close to this in one strand M E317. Blend in straight stitches on top of the leaf with one strand GS 088

and then add some D 3855 to reflect the yellow in the poppies. Use the photo as a guide to placement of colour.

3 Large poppies

Outline the petals using one strand AP 851. Using a blend of one strand each wool and one strand cotton together in the needle, fill each petal with long and short stitch as follows: AP 991 + D blanc, GW 003W3 + D 739, GW 003W4 + D 738, AP 851 + D 3855, then one strand D 3827. Emphasise the dark shadowed areas afterwards using one strand D 977, 3790 in straight stitches. Work the deepest shadows underneath the petals in split stitch using one strand D 3787, then blend in a few straight stitches into this line using one strand D 3790. Use the photo as a guide to colour placement.

4 Poppy centres

Use one strand of cotton throughout. Outline the centre pod with split stitch using D 926 and fill with long and short stitch, shading from light to dark teal across the pod in D 928, 927, 926, 3768, 3799. Finish with dark grey 3799. Work a few small straight stitches along the edge of the pod centre with D 524. Work the centre of the pod with

Stitch direction diagram

French knots in 3799, then work a line of French knots on either side of this with 524 and 522. Stitch the stamens with random straight stitches in 3787, 3371 and then lighter ones in 3827. Work random French knots along the top of and among the stamens in D 3371, 3787, 3827, 3855 (work the darker ones first and build up to the lighter ones).

Use the photo as a guide to colour placement.

5 Pink blossoms

Outline all the petals with split stitch using 2 strands D 3836. Fill each petal, starting with the ones that are furthest back, with long and short stitch, shading from light to dark towards the centre. In the first row use one strand each together in the needle of 3866 + 153, thereafter use 2 strands 3836, 3835, 3834, then change to one strand 3790 to finish. Emphasise the shadowed areas underneath the petals with one strand 3790 by blending in a few straight stitches afterwards as needed. Fill the centre with French knots using one strand each AP 851 + D 3790 together in the needle.

6 Small white/almond blossoms

Fill each petal with straight stitches from the centre out towards the edge, using one strand CW 030 for the front flowers and CW 098 for the back flowers. Work all the stitches into the same hole in the centre and continue building up stitches on top of the previous ones to give a plump look to the petals. Take one strand of D 3836 and 3835 and work alternate straight stitches at the base of each petal. Fill the centre with French knots using a blend of one strand each together in the needle D 3790 + 3371.

7 Large teal green leaves

Fill each leaf with fly stitch using one strand CW 197.

8 Small olive leaves

Fill each leaf with fly stitch using one strand each of wool and cotton together in the needle, of either AP 341 + D 642 or AP 975 + D 640.

9 Stems

Work the large main stems at base in stem stitch using 2 strands D 642 or 640. Work all the remaining stems for buds and grasses in split stitch using 2 strands D 642 or 640.

10 Buds

Outline each bud with split stitch using one strand GW 030. Work a few straight stitches across each bud to provide a bit of padding and work satin stitch in one strand of GW 030 at an angle on top of these.

11 Grasses

Work French knots randomly across the stems using one strand GW 030

BIBLIOGRAPHY

Andrews, Carol, *Embroideries from an English Garden*, 1997, Ruth Bean Publishers, ISBN—13: 978-0903585309

A—Z Thread Painting, 2005, Country Bumpkin Publications, ISBN—13: 978 0975092040

Burr, Trish, 2002, *Redouté's Finest Flowers in Embroidery*, Sally Milner Publishing, ISBN—10: 1863512934
    or ISBN—13: 978 1863512930

Burr, Trish, 2006, *Long and Short Stitch Embroidery: A Collection of Flowers*, Sally Milner Publishing, ISBN—10: 1863513523
    or ISBN—13: 978 1863513524

The World's Most Beautiful Embroidered Blankets, 2004, Country Bumpkin Publications, ISBN 0-9757094-7-X

SUPPLIERS

Trish Burr (South Africa)
Email: erenvale@mweb.co.za

Burford Needlecraft (threads and fabric)
Cheltenham Road
Burford
Oxfordshire OX18 4JA
UK
Tel: +44 1993 822136
Email: info@needlework.co.uk
Website: www.needlework.co.uk

The Caron Collection (Caron threads)
55 Old South Avenue
Stratford CT 06615
USA
Tel: +1 203 381 9999
Email: mail@caron-net.com
Website: www.caron-net.com

**Cascade House Australia
(Cascade House threads)**
86b Albert Street
Creswick Victoria 3363
Australia
Tel: +61 3 5345 1120
Fax: +61 3 5345 2562
Email: info@cascadehouse.com.au
Website: www.cascadehouse.com.au

Chameleon Threads South Africa
Email: info@needlecraft.co.za
Website: www.needlecraft.co.za

**Country Bumpkin Retail Store (Australia)
(all supplies)**
Tel: Australia (08) 8372 7676
Tel: International +61 8 8372 7676
Email: cbretail@countrybumpkin.com.au
Website: www.countrybumpkin.com.au

The Crewel Gobelin (Australia) (all supplies)
9 Marian Street
Killara NSW 2071
Australia
Tel: +61 2 9498 6831
Fax: +61 2 9499 5001
Email: enquiries@thecrewelgobelin.com.au
Website: www.thecrewelgobelin.com.au

DMC (DMC threads and fabrics)
To find your nearest local stockist look on their website:
www.dmc.com

Gloriana Hand-Dyed Threads
15410 NE 157th Street
Woodinville WA 98072
USA
Tel: +1 425 488 0479
Fax: +1 425 488 0480
Email: gloriana1@earthlink.net
Website: www.glorianathreads.com

Gretchen Cagle (decorative painting books)
PO Box 2104
Claremore
OK 74018
USA
Tel: +1 918 342 1080
Fax: +1 918 341 8909
Email: CaglePub@aol.com
Website: www.gretchencagle.com

Gumnut Yarns
PO Box 858
Bathurst NSW 2795
Australia

Tel: +61 2 6332 6771
Fax: +61 2 6332 6774
Email: info@gumnutyarns.com
Website: www.gumnutyarns.com

House of embroidery threads
Email: info@houseofembroidery.com
Website: www.houseofembroidery.com

Thistle Needleworks Inc (all supplies)
1005 Hebron Avenue
Glastonbury CT 06033
USA
Tel: +1 860 633 8503
Fax: +1 860 633 1851
Email: ThisNeedle@aol.com
Website: www.ThistleNeedleworks.com

Twining Thread (all supplies)
255 NW Coast St
PO Box 485
Newport OR 97365
Tel: +1 541 265 2166
Fax: +1 541 265 2164
Email: info@twiningthread.com
Website: www.twiningthread.com